# balance

# balance

betsy de thierry

Published in Great Britain by Grosvenor House Publishing Ltd

www.freedombathandbristol.com

Book and cover design by Nathalia Kirilloff

International Standard Book No ISBN 978-1-78148-638-2

# With Thanks

This book has been written as an attempt to help people. I am grateful to those who have helped me. Thank you so much to my husband, Andrew, who listens to me verbally process for hours on end and to my four boys; Josh, Ben, Jonah and Noah who live an adventurous life with us as we try to follow God on the wiggly path that He leads us on. I pray that you boys will continue to live a life totally focused on the purposes and plans of God whilst having a complete blast.

Thank you too to the team at Freedom Bath and Bristol who are on a wild journey of following God against the culture of religion and mediocrity.

Thank you God that you continue to define, strengthen and prepare us to bring in more of Your Kingdom where darkness currently rules.

Thank you God for never leaving us, being our strength and shield, being the anchor in the storm and the reason we live.

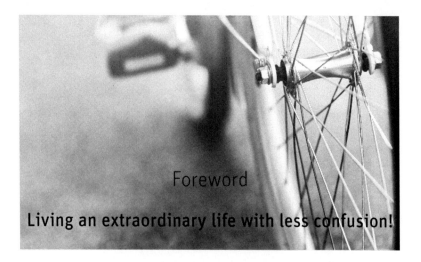

## Foreword

### Living an extraordinary life with less confusion!

There is a Jewish proverb that says we should all carry around two notes in the pockets of our coats. In one pocket the note says 'I am but dust', and in the other pocket a note which says, 'and all the earth is made for me'.

That is what this book is about. As we push on in following Jesus and we study and listen to messages, there are so many seemingly opposing or contradicting truths that were always designed to be held together. This book is an attempt to outline and explore some of these tensions. One truth without the other brings lack of balance As we allow the fusion of truths to be held together there is a power surge of revelation and faith.

The most central message of the Bible is the story of the cross and the story of the resurrection. Really they are the same story but they have often become separated by different emphasis. When they are preached together, the true power of total redemption is extraordinary.

Some people may turn up in church and then hear a message, for example, on making the best use of every second because time is our most powerful and valuable resource. They could leave convicted to stop wasting time and motivated to squeeze all they can out of life. This could be great unless they are already driven and near exhaustion and then that teaching may not be too helpful! They weren't here in church six months ago when the value of the Sabbath and taking time to reflect and rest was preached clearly.

Jesus frequently spoke in paradoxes and invited His listeners to compare one way of life with another and draw their own conclusions. Here in our over-developed Western life we seem to automatically look for formulas and search for black and white answers to life's questions. Yet many other cultures seem better able to naturally embrace two seemingly opposite or conflicting viewpoints and not see them as contradictory. This thinking is like the two pedals of a bike; one pedal pushes down and the other pedal follows, with both pedals needed for movement. A classic example of this would be the verse in Proverbs where there seems to be a blatant contradiction;

*'Don't respond to the stupidity of a fool; you'll only look foolish yourself.*
*Answer a fool in simple terms so he doesn't get a swelled head.'*
**(Proverbs 26:4-5)**

An example of a purposed paradox in the Bible to whet your appetite and make your spiritual tummy rumble is when Jesus is described as the *'Prince of Peace'* (Isaiah 9:6) and yet also says of himself, *'...I did not come to bring peace, but a sword.'* (Matthew 10:34)

Despite the eagerness that I feel as I look at the titles of these chapters, I do feel that it is worth saying that I personally am not someone who enjoys the word 'balance' as it seems to create an image of sensible, practical and quite frankly boring. However, I believe that an ability to explore the paradoxes that are found in the Bible and to grasp theological balance is essential for clarity and maturity, which can lead to an increasingly fruitful life.

Most of us experience the complexity of balances in our daily lives without thinking too much about them. For example, as we parent our kids we know that we can't just bring them up in atmosphere of discipline without demonstrating love in action because the children will feel unloved and afraid. We balance love and discipline to empower our kids for the best possible future.

These chapters are messages that I have preached in our church to try and help the people build healthy theological foundations, in order to see them live lives full of purpose and become the extraordinary people that they have been created to be. Each chapter is written as a study aid and as such there are Bible references provided at the end of every chapter.

It should settle your heart and excite your spirit!

# Contents

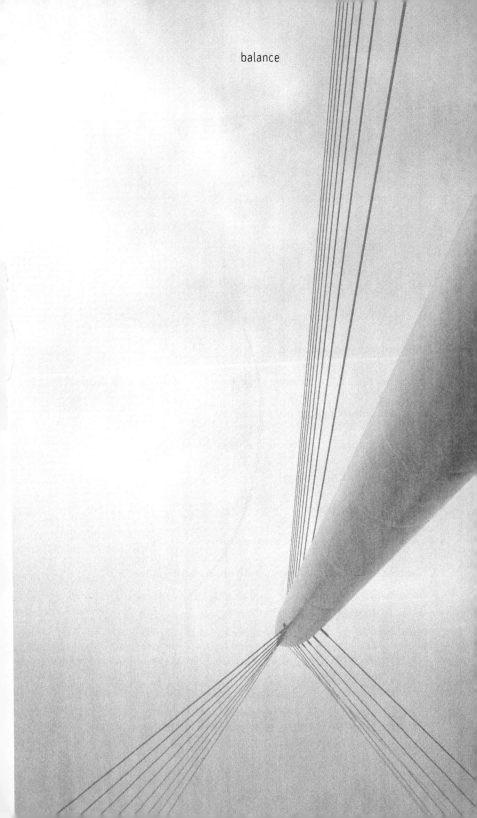

balance

# Chapter 1

## God as the All Consuming Fire and our Father

One of the most amazing things about knowing God is that He is both the lover of our souls and the Lion of Judah. (Revelation 5:5) He is as much an eternal judge as our greatest advocate. He wants to be the best friend we've ever had and yet holds the nations as drops of water in a bucket (Isaiah 40:15). These seem to be incompatible truths and yet they are not. It's the combination of these seemingly opposing characteristics that makes the good news of Jesus so powerful. To truly follow Jesus we are people who want to commit to the journey of holding and treasuring all these extraordinary truths.

As people who follow Jesus our main goal is to 'know Him', not just know about Him. He is beyond description and above our comprehension but the more revelation we have of Him, the more we love Him. Let's take a look at some of these truths and allow them to sink into our hearts, as we enjoy the adventure of holding His power, majesty and intimate overwhelming love in each hand.

### A holy awe of God

God has to be God. He has to be beyond our human understanding otherwise He is merely a fellow colleague, a peer or a good example. Comforting though those things are, they are not sufficient for us to desire His will and His ways before anything.

As we begin to grasp God's extraordinary power and love we are compelled to worship with awe the creator God, who describes Himself as 'I am who I am'. No name can hold the depths of who God is; He is beyond description. His power, might and strength are mind-blowing. The only suitable reaction to pondering on His nature is one of reverence and awe. To tremble at His name and to quake at the thought of His presence is appropriate. He holds the power of judge. The mountains quake at the sound of His voice, which is the sound of mighty waters. He lifts up the islands like fine dust and His breath changes everything. To see Him is to die. We are encouraged to magnify Him as we focus on Him being beyond our understanding. The bigger He becomes in our thinking, the more we trust Him with our whole lives.

We need to carve out time in our busy lives to remember that we are but dust and that God can, with one breath, shatter all our human plans and efforts if He so chose. This shouldn't make us afraid, but fill us with an appropriate awe for his power. In our contemporary culture, all too often our young people are growing up being taught that God is their best friend without any teaching on His power, awe and holiness. It seems that people are nervous that we might scare the little children, but I believe they need to have understanding of his power, majesty and love.

There is a culture that has become prevailing in Western Christian churches, where we are so desperate for people to experience the beauty, comfort and life awakening love of God, that there seems to be some fear of teaching the true Holiness of God. So churches become full of people who are really worshipping Father Christmas, but they haven't noticed! They are worshipping a man many people don't believe in, that they can't see, who gives them presents and makes them feel full of hope. They enjoy the community experience of believing in the tale, as their desire for love is so strong that it holds the community together in unity.

Does this sound like church?

It shouldn't! Church should have a serious understanding of the power and majesty of God that doesn't dilute His love but deepens it.

The church seems happy to acknowledge God as a God of justice when it comes to the slaves and the hungry but is uncomfortable learning about the God of justice when there is any application to our own day to day lives. Our western church seems to like to argue against the theology that God has rules that we need to honour, with consequences if we don't. There seems to be disbelief in the justice of God being applicable to our own lives and the corporate community of church. Yet I see God's justice as an expression of His love. I know I am loving with my little children when I shout 'No!' loudly as their tiny fingers go towards the fire. It's a loud, probably scary shout and declaration to try and keep the little ones safe.

It is appropriate to feel overwhelmed by God's power but not frightened;

small and tiny but not belittled; awed but excited.

**God as the lover of our soul**
Yet the same God, creator, Lord, Lion of Judah, Judge of the living and the dead is our saviour. He knows us intimately and loves us deeply. He knows our limitations, weaknesses, frailty and sin and yet He cherishes us individually. God rejoices over us with singing and knows our names, our thoughts, our heart's intentions, our desires and our fears. Our hair is numbered and His love for us is constant and unwavering (Matthew 10:30).

As we focus on God as kind, loving and approachable we are drawn into a relationship with Him. We desire to be with the One who knows our thoughts before we think them and our words before we say them. He is familiar with the depths of our heart and yet remains constant in His love for us.

God knitted us together in our mother's womb, whether we were planned or wanted by our parents (Psalm 139:13). He chose us. He planned for us. He made us. He watches over us and longs for us to know this love. God is love and in his perfect love, fear is cast out (1 John 4:18). His love envelops, and comforts. His love is sufficient to carry us through the darkest days. His love is whiter than snow, purer than anything we have experienced, with no hidden agendas, deception, twisting or evil intent. God's love is all we crave in our deepest place; our hearts need to experience His love in our brokenness. His love pours like healing oil into our broken hearts and brings relief. It takes the sting of pain out and heals the most fragile wound. His love flows so constantly and powerfully towards us. If only we would stop to allow Him to love us and to experience His love. We need to wait in His presence; wait patiently before Him.

His love is so unlike anything we have or will ever experience on this earth. The Bible expresses His love in various stories and various ways to try and describe it.

*'The Lord God is in your midst, a victorious warrior. He will exult over you with joy, He will quieten you with His love, He will rejoice over you with singing.'* **(Zephaniah 3:17)**

*'Since you are precious and honoured in my sight, since you are honoured and I love you...'* **(Isaiah 43:4)**

If we try and compare His love to anything we have ever experienced on this earth, we will never even expect to know something so extraordinary. No human will ever be able to love the way that He who is Love does.

Many of us base our understanding of love on the best experience of love that we have had. For many people that would be the love of their mother or father. Yet this love is nothing compared to the powerful, extraordinary, restoring, beautiful love of God. We need to allow God to work through our experiences of parental love, no matter how good it has been, so that we can see where God's love is different. For those of us who have been hurt by those who were meant to care for us and protect us, it is even more important to process our pasts so that they don't affect our relationship with God. His love teaches us how to really love those around us.

### Understanding God as loving, compassionate, merciful and also a God of Justice who is not 'nice'.

I used to confuse God's love with God being nice. To be nice is to be pleasant, relatively neutral and not in any way passionate or transformation bringing. An average UK citizen is quite nice. It's a very neutral stance. God does not value this gospel of niceness. His love is a fiery, protective love. This love is full of healing power, comfort and tenderness at the same time as He values justice and His word being honoured and obeyed. Often if God asks us to do something which is perceived to be not nice yet Biblical, like challenging someone, it feels uncomfortable. To challenge someone is often seen as intimidating or even manipulating as an adult, yet as a young adult in university culture it's quite acceptable. So what stops challenge being loving in adulthood? Is it pride that stops us seeing it as an expression of real love, where we desire each other to know the truth so that the truth will set us free?

I used to think that God wanted me to please everyone, and being as 'nice' as possible proved spirituality and closeness to God. This was the Christian culture I was raised in. However, in the last few years it has been painful and agonising to be attacked and slandered by various broken people and be viewed as not nice as I have tried to obey God. This has led me to discover, in the deep place of my heart, that God's love was not conditional on people being pleased with me. I had to discover in my heart, not just in my head, that God knew my heart and the attempts to discredit me were from the enemy. It has been a time of breakthrough as I have slowly become more released from the need to be seen as 'nice' which I had subconsciously believed was a badge of being a Christian. I was able to exchange this lie with knowledge that Jesus was not seen as nice, but a man of righteousness, justice, mercy, grace and truth. My perspective on my identity and ability to follow Jesus has significantly changed, as I was able to embrace this new revelation. (There is more about this in Chapter 8).

God is both the King of Kings and the Lord of Lords. As creator and author of life, the whole earth will bow the knee to Him. He is also the lover of our soul and our daddy (Abba Father. Mark 14:36) who sings over us and knows us intimately. We must learn to hold both truths as equal and vital. This is the good news! Let us not try and put God into a box and decide who He is. We can grow in our relationship with Him as we spend time with Him. We need to constantly choose Him over other distractions and plan to get to know Him. However, human kind will never be able to comprehend the mind or ways of God and He will always surprise us (1 Corinthians 2:11). The journey of relationship with God is learning to trust Him, depend on Him and follow His lead, even when we know we don't understand His timing, His ways and His thoughts.

It becomes a relief when we allow God to be God and stop trying to understand Him. I am reminded of my youngest son who tries so hard to understand and be a part of his older brothers' interests. He uses some of the right words and tries to be cool, but somehow it always ends up just sounding cute. This frustrates him endlessly. I have noticed that in his frustration he is cross, gets upset and maybe even begins to show signs of anxiety that he doesn't have the same level of understanding. It's only when we remind him of his position in the family as one where we want to protect and nurture him, until he is ready to understand, does he relax, snuggle up and enjoy being 'the little one'. This seems so similar when we look at how our finite minds must function in contrast to God's mind and understanding. It's only when we relax and enjoy our position that we can go on our journey with a lightness and excitement in our spirit rather than an anxiety and nervousness that we are not fully in control. It's only when we remind ourselves of how vast, enormous and powerful our God is, that we laugh at our own anxiety and desire to control our lives. Just as our youngest cannot cook for himself, wash his clothes, earn money or be responsible for his daily living, in the same way it is ridiculous to think we can be in a position to understand the mind of God. We can, however know what He reveals to us and snuggle up in the comfort of His love and care for us all individually.

Let us remember to pray as Jesus taught us starting with an acknowledgement of the father heart of God alongside the majesty of God.

> *'Our Father who is in heaven, Hallowed be your name.'*
> **(Matthew 6:9)**

**A question and some Bible verses to study:**
Question: How do we keep holding the focus of God being both so Holy and majestic and yet relate to Him as our father?

> *'...His voice was like the sound of many waters...do not be afraid I am the first and the last'.* **(Revelation 1:1-17)**

> *'I heard a voice from heaven, like the sound of many waters and like the sound of loud thunder...'* **(Revelation 14: 2)**

> *'For our God is an all consuming fire.'* **(Hebrews 12:29)**

> *'...Our Father who is in heaven, Hallowed be your name'*
> **(Matthew 6:9)**

> *'I will not leave you as orphans; I will come to you.'* **(John 14:18)**

*'Behold the nations are like a drop from a bucket, and are regarded as a speck of dust on the scales; behold he holds up the islands like fine dust.'* **(Isaiah 40:15)**

*'In the year that King Uzziah's death, I saw the Lord sitting in a throne, lofty and exalted, with the train of his robe filling the temple. Seraphim stood above Him, each having six wings; with two he covered his face, with two he covered his feet and with two he flew. And one called out to another and said, 'Holy Holy Holy is the lord of hosts, the whole earth is full of His glory.' The foundations of the thresholds trembled at the voice of him who called out, while the temple was filled with smoke. Then I said,' woe to me, for I am ruined! Because I am a man of unclean lips....'* **(Isaiah 6:1-5)**

*'Like a shepherd He will tend His flock, In His arms He will gather the lambs and carry them close to His heart.'* **(Isaiah 40:11)**

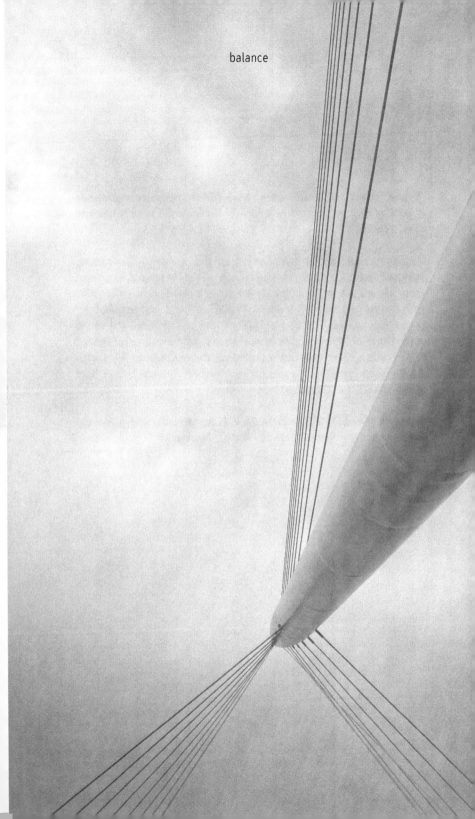

balance

# Chapter 2

## Humble servants and royal rulers

One of the primary revelations that we grasp as followers of Jesus is that of our identity as His children. As we have increased revelation and become more confident in who the Bible says that we are, we are completely transformed.

**Knowing that we are children of the King of Kings**
So many people suffer from a bad self-image and consequently spend their time striving to prove themselves in order to receive affirmation, and so it is the most amazing revelation to realise that when we give our lives back to Jesus we become God's adopted children. No longer do we need to struggle with who we are or feel competitive about the people around us because we can feel secure in the knowledge that we are chosen and valued. We can learn to listen to the voice of the One who has words of life to speak to us. We can learn to love ourselves as we are. We care about the audience of one, Jesus!

**Walking with authority and confidence**
We are called as children of the King of Kings to walk in His authority to bring the kingdom of heaven on this earth. We are His ambassadors (2 Corinthians 5:20) and as such have been given His name, His assignments, His authority, and a position of power. We are given the mind of Christ (1 Corinthians 2:16) and are called to become increasingly like Him in our character as our mind is renewed (Romans 12:2). We are royalty (1 Peter 2:9), adopted into the family of the King of Kings, (Ephesians1: 5) where we are His heirs (Romans 8:17). We are positioned as powerful, influential, world changing rulers who can trample on serpents (Luke 10:19) and see supernatural miracles happen where others are powerless. That is some identity!

We as followers of Jesus have been commissioned as the head and not the tail (Deuteronomy 28:13). We are called to be influential people and atmosphere changers. We have a clear mission. We are called to see people healed of diseases, the dead raised, the broken hearted restored, the desperate become full of hope and faith and the lost become full of purpose and vision.

We are an incredible people. We are the most confident people on earth when we allow God to reveal to us His thoughts about us. We are children of the King of Kings! Our Dad who rules over everything loves us.

It's no longer a situation of priest and laity, with a hierarchical order of those who can hear and co-labour with the King of Kings and those who are untouchables. Now we are all called priests (1 Peter 2:9). We all have access to the presence of the most powerful God of all time. We are God's children and can walk with boldness to His throne, talk to Him freely and know Him (Hebrews 4:16).

### Bold and trusting
Once I was studying the word 'garments' in the Bible and started to realise how much God wanted to reveal to us. I was pondering how people hide themselves in their clothing and can mask their real selves. The Bible tells us that God has prepared for us a white robe of righteousness that covers us with His purity and mercy. This garment is not to cover up our real selves but to actually cause us to transform from the inside out as Jesus' blood cleanses us. We are then seen as white and pure by God as we are 'in Christ'.

I studied other garments and found that the colour red was a symbol of victory. I like to think that when we face troubles and difficulties, if we wear the red garment of victory we can overcome. This garment has written all over it stories of answers to prayer, stories of Gods faithfulness and goodness, and other peoples stories and testimonies. This red testimony garment carries us through the tough times as we meditate on God's goodness and faithfulness and the blood of Jesus that has set us free. Then we can choose to wear the purple garment of royalty. The story in Ezekiel 16 of a young girl who was rescued while she was lying in her blood, abandoned and dying, is a metaphor for our salvation. In the story she is adopted and is made a member of the royal household and adorned with gifts. In our story we are adopted into the King's household and we become children of the King of Kings and Lord of Lords. As we choose to put on our royal garment we walk in a new way, with a new boldness because of who our father is. We need to choose to remember these garments. (There is more about these garments and the colours in one of my other books, 'Making Your mess Your Message.')

As I was studying these garments, I was pondering on hiding and the need people have to protect themselves from rejection and interpersonal pain. As I was sleeping one night I heard an audible whisper and the word, 'Batach'. I wrote it down and the next day looked it up. The definition of this Hebrew word in Strong's concordance of the Bible is; 'to hide, in boldness, confidence, surety and trust'. The word bold is the same word used only one other time in Proverbs 28:1:

> 'The wicked flee, though no one pursues, but the righteous are bold like a lion.'

I realized in a divine intervention that God never wanted us to hide in fear, or shame or nervousness but in confidence and boldness. I realized again that whilst I had sung many times of God being a strong tower for me to run into and be safe, I had pictured myself hiding, feeling nervous and unsure. This is wrong. God wants us to know that when we know our identity as His children we can hide in boldness and confidence while He protects our vulnerability.

**Being the greatest servant**
We are people filled with his power and aware of our identity and purpose. We know that we are royalty and wherever we go we change atmospheres and cause a reaction. We are also called to be the greatest servants of all, who recognise the grace that God has shown us by adopting us as His own, and lavishing us with His love and empowering us to live. We need to hold these two revelations in our hands at the same time.

We are people who have been called to serve the world in the same way that Jesus served the world. We are told to serve one another in love, preferring others and sacrificing our comfort for theirs. Jesus was the greatest servant of all despite His position, power and authority. He demonstrated how He put aside His comfort to love others. He models a servant attitude by continually healing and teaching people. We see Him washing the feet of His disciples in John 13. He says in John 12:26, '... *anyone who serves Me, the Father will honour.*'

If we don't remember this as we meditate on our position as the children of the King of Kings, we will surely become proud, arrogant and treat others as servants. Whilst we are the children of the King of Kings, we are also His followers and disciples, and therefore we don't focus on ourselves but on God Himself as we deny ourselves to serve His purposes.

We then realise that we don't need to compete against each other for popularity, as we read that Jesus wasn't popular, and we don't need to live for affirmation from other people but aim to please our heavenly father.

We don't compete to be the most influential or have the most impressive breadth of ministry as God is responsible for the breadth, and we are only responsible for the depth. It's our job to ensure integrity and a teachable spirit that longs for God's rule, and it is His role to send us to where He has planned for us. It doesn't matter where we go and what we do, it only matters whether we are being obedient and whether our motivation is to please Him. We try and trust and obey, knowing that there is no other way!

### Walking in humility

I have noticed that we are often told in the Bible that we need to choose to be humble. Sometimes people seem to imply that being humble is a state of self-hatred and self-slandering. This negative stance has been accepted and has sometimes been encouraged behaviour for some centuries, amongst Christians, yet that is not the definition of humble. To be humble doesn't mean that we walk around, heads drooping, ashamed of our sin and brokenness. Humble means that we know who we are in relation to God and are totally dependent on Him for our life.

It's never nice when we read a story in the Old Testament about God humbling a nation because the words 'defeat', 'destroy' and 'pain' are usually associated with it. We are clearly instructed to make a choice to remember who we are in the context of our own ability compared to God's and remember who gave us those abilities. When we put the facts on the table it doesn't take very long to remember that we are nothing without Him. God gives us the air to breathe! The fragility of life is easily forgotten in our busyness, until someone dies unexpectedly and then we remember to be grateful for the breath we breathe. It's important to remember that it is God who gave us our breath, life, gifts, and all that we have belongs to him. When we live from the position that we haven't earned a thing and when we remember that everything good has come from Him, we are in a safe place.

Jesus asks us to remember our weakness and not be ashamed of it. We need to be reminded that anything we do of value is due to God's grace in our weakness. We are called to humble ourselves and ensure that we don't think of ourselves more highly than we ought (Romans 12:3). This is because the power of God is perfected in our weakness (2 Corinthians 12:9-10) not in our sin, but in our recognition of our humanity and tendency towards sin and self. As we serve others and remember the grace of God towards us, we will ensure that we keep central in our minds that God is the source of everything and we are just His servants, fulfilling His assignments.

I often think of my experiences of making cakes with my children. When they were little I bought the ingredients, weighed them and the children carefully tipped them into the bowl. I prepared the tins and put the oven on. The children tipped and stirred. I usually had to re-do the stirring as it wasn't quite enough. I then cleaned up the mess knowing that if I had done this on my own it would have been both quicker and cleaner. This is how I feel about us doing God's work! I feel that God could do it far quicker and cleaner without us, but He has chosen us to share the experience. When we do something well, we feel a sense of pleasure. In the same way I love to hear the children express their delight too in their cake making and I enjoy the experience of seeing the pride on their faces. God loves the delight on our faces when we manage to run a church service or pray for a neighbour. He is proud of us whilst knowing that without Him, we can do nothing of eternal worth.

Others may think that we are being arrogant when we are confident. They don't see that we are confident because of our recognition of our dependence on Gods power, grace and love. This is why people make mistakes when they judge others using external sights. It doesn't work. Who knows what is going on in someone's heart unless they speak? There is a huge difference between arrogance and confidence. Arrogance is the reliance on, and belief in, our own skills, strength and power whilst a healthy Biblical confidence is a boldness that comes from knowing that God's power is at work in our lives. Then we know that nothing is too difficult for Him. We are unstoppable, influential and powerful because of the grace of God. It's easier to remember our total dependence on God when we start out, but we need to constantly remember that our successes and triumphs are because of Him.

Romans 12:16 in The Message Bible sums it up beautifully;

*'Get along with each other, don't be stuck up. Make friends with nobodies and don't be the great somebody.'*

Royalty is my identity and servanthood is my assignment.

### A question and some verses to study:
Question: How do we stay or move into a position of humility and servanthood and yet be people who are bold, confident and walk with authority?

*'Think of yourselves the way Christ Jesus thought of himself. He had equal status with God but didn't think so much of himself that he had to cling to the advantages of that status no matter what. Not at all. When the time came, he set aside all the privileges of deity and took on the status of slave, became human. He stayed human. It was an incredibly humbling process. He didn't claim special privileges. Instead he lived a selfless obedient life and then dies a selfless obedient death...'* **(Philippians 2:5-8 The Message)**

*..if being in a community of the spirit means anything to you, if you have a heart, if you care- then do me a favour, be deep spirited friends. Don't push yourselves to the front; don't sweet -talk your way to the top. Put yourself aside, and help others get ahead.'* **(Philippians 2:3 The Message)**

'Be devoted to one another in brotherly love, give preference to one another in honour...' **(Romans 12:10)**

'...The one who is greatest among you must become like the youngest, and the leader like a servant.' **(Luke 22:26)**

'...Through love, serve one another.' **(Galatians 5:13)**

'When people saw the confidence of Peter and John and saw that they were uneducated and untrained men, they were amazed and began to recognise them as having been with Jesus.' **(Acts 4:13)**

'...Most gladly then I will gladly boast about my weaknesses, so that the power of Christ may dwell in me...For when I am weak, then I am strong.' **(2 Corinthians 12:9-10)**

'...Clothe yourself with humility toward one another, for God is opposed to the proud, but gives grace to the humble.' **(1 Peter 5:5)**

'...I dwell in the high and lofty place and with him who has a humble and contrite spirit.' **(Isaiah 57:15)**

'You are no longer a slave, but a son, and if a son an heir through God. **(Galatians 4:7)**

'The Lord will make you the head and not the tail'. **(Deuteronomy 28:13)**

'You are a chosen race, a royal priesthood, a holy nation, a people for Gods own possession , so that you may proclaim the excellencies of Him who has called you out of darkness into His marvellous light.' **(1 Peter 2:9)**

'I can do all things through Him who strengthens me' **(Philippians 4:13)**

*Truly, truly I say to you, he who believes in Me, the works that I do, he will do also; and greater works than these he will do, because I go to my Father.'* **(John 14:12-13)**

*'... We have the mind of Christ.'* **(1 Corinthians 2:16)**

balance

# Chapter 3

## Faith and blessing, suffering and trials

Here's one that seems to trip so many people up in their journey with God. So many followers of Jesus end up confused and disappointed through a lack of this balance so let's explore and grasp the truth as we look at the promises of God, suffering and outrageous blessing! We preach confidently that we are the most blessed people on the planet and we are indeed! We have God on our side, all of heaven cheering us on, and the power of God working in us. We have the creator of the universe singing and rejoicing over us, loving us, knowing us and pursuing us. We are loved, chosen, adopted, adored, understood, cherished, sought after and favoured.

With God for us and not against us, we really are the most blessed people alive.

We know our purpose, our destiny and our identity. He is with us all the time, will never leave us and plans and guides our steps. We'll be with Him forever.

When we pray, things happen. God is waiting to answer our prayer. It's fantastic to hear story after story of miracles all over the world and in our own church communities. In church, we often see people praying and legs growing, backs straightening and cancers leaving. We love to visit people in hospital who were dying, pray for them and see them sit up in bed within a few hours. We love to see the power of God work miracles that are beyond human reasoning!

My family and I have personally known the blessing of God as He has provided extraordinary houses and finance for us miraculously. We currently live in a house that is a miracle because within five weeks of being asked to leave yet another rented house, we were given a load of money and got a mortgage, which we shouldn't have been given! We are now in the process of moving again eight years later and God has taken us on an extraordinary journey of relocating four children to a new area, with new schools and a new house. We have had an amazing time seeing God guide us each step of the way with amazing provision and guidance as each step has unfolded. God has the best plans for us as a family and knows our every specific and detailed need. Every day we are aware of His goodness to us, the power of prayer and the reality of miracles!

It's so important for us expect miracles and supernatural blessings to take place in our lives. I also think it is so vital for our children to be encouraged in  their childlike faith. Jesus told us to show faith like theirs. (Matthew 18:3) We love to let the kids pray and see healing happen such as legs growing in front of them and scars disappearing. We live as ambassadors of a kingdom of miracles, power and supernatural reality.

Those of us who follow Jesus first came to Him by faith, now follow Jesus by faith and live by faith each day. Faith should increase in our lives day by day, month by month, year by year as we live beyond our comfort, reaching out to others and seeing heaven come to earth as we depend on Him, obey Him and follow him. Faith takes us into a life of miracles, intimacy with Jesus, and pleasing Him. The Bible says that *without faith it is impossible to please God*' (Hebrews 11:6). In fact we can see that faith is an essential foundation for everything else to be built upon.

> '*The fundamental fact of existence is that this trust in God, this faith, is the firm foundation under everything that makes life worth living… By faith we see the world called into existence by God's word, what we see created by what we don't see.*' **(Hebrews 11:1-3 The Message)**

Our faith grows each time we see God answer prayer and we see the resulting miracles and signs and wonders. It becomes strengthened as we hold our conviction of things hoped for and things not yet seen (Hebrews 11:1). We are blessed people who are called to bring a message of life and hope to those around us as we experience the wild adventure of a life following Jesus.

> '*…I have come that you may have life and life in all its fullness.*' **(John 10:10)**

**Suffering and trials**

As followers of Jesus whilst we are indeed the most blessed people on the planet who can see miracles happen each and every day, we also are warned not to be surprised at the problems we may suffer. We live in the tension between the kingdom here and the kingdom not yet.

The sufferings, trials and problems that we face are not meant to shake our faith or even cause us alarm, but should strengthen our resolve to fight the battles on earth as part of the winning side. The war was won when Jesus died and rose again. Now we battle against our own carnality and the battles that the enemy throws at us to wear us down, but our faith will carry us through and see us victorious and undefeated!

In 1 Peter 1 we are reminded that tough times can be really helpful in aiming to become more like Jesus.

> '...even though you have to have to put up with every kind of aggravation in the meantime. Pure gold put in the fire comes out of it proved pure; genuine faith put through this suffering comes out proved genuine. When Jesus wraps this all up, its your faith, not your gold, that God will have on display as evidence of his victory.'
> **(1 Peter 1:6-7 The Message)**

We are assured that we will walk through the 'valley of the shadow of death', which is mentioned in Psalm 23. The good news is that we do not have to camp there, hopeless and afraid. We walk through and get safely to the other side. In fact in Revelation chapters 2 and 3 there are many promises from God for 'those who overcome' and so we need to fight these battles in order to develop strength and produce the fruits of the Holy Spirit. It would be impossible for us to become like Jesus and know holiness if everything was simple and easy for us.

In the book of Judges there is a story about the Israelites and how God actually wanted some of the soldiers to fight, even though they didn't have to, because he wanted them to learn in experience what they would never learn in theory and stories only. He actually plans the battle to strengthen and train the young soldiers. The young men needed experience in battles in order to develop skills that could not be formed in theory. It's the same for all of us today.

> 'These are the nations that God left there, using them to test the
> Israelites who had no experience in the Canaanite wars. He did it to
> train the descendants of Israel, the ones who had no battle experience
> in the art of war.... They were there to test Israel and see whether they
> would obey God's commands that were given to their parents through
> Moses.' **(Judges 1:1-4)**

When we go through these difficulties we can know an intimacy and
friendship with God that we could never learn in simple times. This
lesson alone is worth the trials. To experience the strength and protection
of God in the midst of suffering and pain is a beautiful and sacred season.

> ... 'Do not fear for I have redeemed you; I have called you by name;
> you are Mine! When you pass through the waters, I will be with you;
> and through the rivers they will not overflow you. When you walk
> through the fire you will not be scorched, nor will the flame burn you.'
> **(Isaiah 43:1-2)**

There can be many reasons that God allows suffering. It is important to
remember that God is not the author of evil for our lives but allows it to
come sometimes for many reasons. That is not an excuse to sit back, give
in to the problems and be depressed. We are destined to fight, learn and
stand in our authority, exercising our faith to the end. Whilst we live on
this earth, we don't always know the reasons for the hardships, but we
can trust Him that as we fight we are learning lessons and developing
character that is essential to us eternally.

My family have seen pain and suffering and miracles and extraordinary
answers to prayer. My eldest son Josh had a skin problem when he was
about 8 and the Doctor told him it would remain uncomfortable for at
least 5 years. He prayed with faith and learnt to fight, and the skin cleared
up completely within a few weeks. So many times we have prayed about
problems with friends, financial provision and other needs and seen
miracles, which can't be denied.

We also had to pull through the trauma of losing our twin babies who died just before birth and our eldest two sons had to go on that journey with us as we faced the lack of a miracle. But in all situations we have known the presence of God and the comfort of His presence. I won't let any experience that I have faced change what I know is the truth in the word of God. I choose to hold onto the knowledge that I am a mere human whilst God is majestic and awesome and some things I will only understand when I'm in heaven with Him.

So again, let's be people that can walk boldly into our future knowing that we are so blessed to have God guide, love, father, protect and nurture us. It's also good to remember that whilst we live in this earth and our role is to bring the rule of heaven onto earth, there will be trials and difficulties. Let's stop getting so shocked when things are tough, but remember how good God is and walk through the valleys knowing they won't last forever as God walks before us to prepare our way. His mercy and goodness follow us all the days of our life and He never leaves us or forsakes us, but is with us always no matter what happens! Let's use every experience to help us become more like Jesus.

**A question and some Bible verses to study:**
Question: How can we be people of faith whilst also holding in balance that we are not meant to be surprised when trials come our way?

'We have this treasure in earthen vessels, so that the surpassing greatness of the power will be of God and not from ourselves. We are afflicted in every way, but not crushed, perplexed but not despairing, persecuted but not forsaken, struck down but not destroyed.'
**(2 Corinthians 4:7)**

'...If God is for us who can be against us?' **(Romans 8:31)**

'...All things work together for those who love him.' **(Romans 8:28)**

'But we in all things conquer through Him who loved us.'
**(Romans 8:37)**

'Whatever God has promised gets stamped with the Yes of Jesus.'
**(2 Corinthians 1:20)**

' No weapon that's formed against me will prosper.' **(Isaiah 54:17)**

'No evil will befall me neither shall plague come nigh my dwelling.'
**(Psalm 91:10)**

'The Lord has pleasure in the prosperity of His people.' **(Psalm 35:27)**

'You are from God little children and have overcome them; because
greater is He who is in you than He who is in the world.'
**(1 John 4:4)**

Consider it pure joy when you encounter various trials, knowing that
the testing of your faith produces endurance. And let endurance have
its perfect result, so that you may be perfect, lacking in nothing.'
**(James 1:2-4)**

'Blessed is a man who perseveres under trial, for once he has been
approved, he will receive the crown of life which the Lord has promised
to those who love him.' **(James 1:12)**

'You will be hated by all because of my name.' **(Matthew 10:22)**

'Indeed, all who desire to live godly in Christ Jesus will be persecuted.'
**(2 Timothy 3:12)**

Suffer hardship with me as a good soldier of Christ Jesus...for this
reason I endure all things for the sake of those who are being chosen...'
**(2 Timothy 2:3-10)**

balance

# Chapter 4

## Forgetting, remembering and dealing with the past

In the book of Philippians we are told clearly to 'forget what lies behind and reach forward to what lies ahead... I press on toward the goal'. (Philippians 3:13-14) It is indeed important to focus on the future and all the things that God has prepared for us. It's such good news that Gods mercies are 'new every morning' (Lamentations 3:22-23). We all need and long for nothing more than the new start that God promises us.

We live a life full of purpose as followers of Jesus and recognise that God has planned assignments on earth for us to achieve, as we co-labour with Him to bring heaven onto earth. It is clear that He directs us to press into our future and rid ourselves of all the things that can stop us being free to run into that which he has prepared for us. It says in Ephesians 2:10:

> 'We are His workmanship, created in Christ Jesus for good works, which God prepared beforehand so that we would walk in them.'

We live a purpose driven life, excited about our destiny, with our eyes fixed on Jesus. (Hebrews 12:1-2) We know that as we look forward we are preparing ourselves to be available to all that God asks of us and are free to be excited and envisioned;

> 'Brethren I do not regard myself as having laid hold of it and yet; but one thing I do; forgetting what lies behind and reaching forward to what lies ahead. I press on toward the goal for the prize of the upward call of God in Christ Jesus.' **(Philippians 3:13-14)**

The picture we are presented with in Philippians is one of an athlete being disciplined to concentrate on the goal ahead. The goal that we are meant to be focusing all our energy on, in this race of life, is to Know Him, not just know about Him. The things that can stop us knowing Him, because they can weigh us down and distort our perceptions, can be issues of guilt and regret over past mistakes and times when others have hurt us.

We all know what it is like to have an argument on the way to a party and be so full of hurt or regret that the event can be tainted. Life is not meant to be lived under the influence of negative past memories or with the pain of unresolved loss and confusion. The good news is that Jesus died that we can be healed from the consequences of other's sin towards us and live free from the guilt of our own sin. As we forgive those who have hurt us we can choose to allow Him to heal us and we can know freedom from emotional pain. As we repent of any mistakes made, we can know freedom from the power and weight of guilt. We can feel free to run towards Jesus with boldness and confidence.

Jesus does indeed give us a brand new start.

**Integrity of heart**
We also have a responsibility to allow God to transform us from the inside out. People often try and change their behaviour from being dysfunctional to more functional, to become more like Jesus or just a better person. Often they can hit resistance, which they can't always understand. We change when the Holy Spirit works on the inside of us and by the renewing of our minds. There is a mental decision that needs to be continually made in the process of change but it doesn't stop there. Integrity can only be truly achieved when the heart, mind and spirit are aligned and integrated. When the heart is wounded it acts separately to the mind. It breeds conflict that is sometimes not voiced but can be seen in our behaviour.

If we were to deny our pasts and just declare over them, 'I am a new creation the old is past and the new has come' (2 Corinthians 5:17), we would be denying God the opportunity to bring real truth and healing and instead we would be opting for a life of pretence. Sometimes God does heal us in an instant and whole experiences are resolved in prayer that would take so long to psychologically process. This is my prayer, that we would see more and more of these supernatural interventions of healing from past trauma. For some people though, it is helpful to have a skilled person help them and guide them through some of the internal difficulties. God has designed us to be in relationship and be interdependent. I was raised in an environment where mental illness was seen as failure as a Christian. The church had no compassion or empathy to offer those in mental turmoil, only judgement, fear and pity. These days there seems to be more love and understanding. It is important to be people who are full of compassion; prayerful and expectant that God will bring supernatural healing to all inner turmoil and pain. He is the Healer of the broken hearted and in His presence there is healing.

**God as The Healer**
When we have been hurt by events and experiences in our past, we must try not to run away from them or project them onto someone else. Projection is a defence mechanism in which unwanted feelings are displaced onto another person. It is a clever but unhelpful way for someone to deal with difficulty through being in denial and then subconsciously or consciously transferring guilt for their own thoughts, emotions and actions onto another person as a way of avoiding having to face the guilt. It is amazing how common this defensive, protective behaviour is, but it is damaging to relationships and communities as it's based on deception. It's also not nice for the person being projected onto. Let's be sensitive to God showing us when we are projecting and instead take the pain to Him to heal rather than blame someone else. Jesus told us to inspect our own hearts and not make judgements about other people. (Matthew 7:3 -5)

There are lots of different ways of avoiding strong feelings of guilt and shame and God knows all about our defence mechanisms and our ways of coping, and He wants us to be honest. Let's be people who ask God to shine the light on our hearts and take responsibility for our actions.

Let's face these hurts and allow God to heal us. If we don't do this there is a high chance that these old, past wounds can affect our behaviour and our attitudes. God loves to heal the broken hearted and set the captive free (Isaiah 61). Healing our heart is a vital part of His desire to enable us to become all that He planned for us. As God heals our hearts, this enables us to leave pain and disappointment in the past rather than carry it as sacks of hidden hurt all our lives. God knows that we need healing from things that happen to us and so He gave us the good news that it is

Jesus who came to heal our broken hearts. It is Jesus who can take us out of captivity that we have become locked into. Whatever situation you are currently facing, whatever hurt that is right now festering and leaking poison in your soul, whatever wound that hurts, God is able to heal and bring transformation and restoration.

If God was able to create us out of dust, he can reform a broken heart. If God made our brains to be resilient enough that we can create defence mechanisms and systems to keep us alive in the midst of a nightmare, then He is also able to heal and bring rest to the internal world of a traumatised person.

After all, God created the brain and He knows that it can be easy to get stuck in the survival mode, 'fight, flight and freeze' due to constant trauma but God is able to re order these parts of our brains and bring rest and relief to the whole body.

Nothing is too big for God to deal with and nothing can rock His boat or knock Him off His throne. His kingdom lasts forever and his healing will always be available to those who ask and wait in his presence.

> '*The spirit of the Lord God is upon me, because the Lord has anointed me to bring good news to the afflicted. He has sent me to bind up the broken hearted, to proclaim liberty to captives and freedom to prisoners.*' **(Isaiah 61:1-2)**

**Meditating on the past**
We need to allow the Holy Spirit to bring back to our memory past wounds and hurts which are affecting our present behaviour so that He can heal us and set us free. We also need to remember and think about all the answered prayer, the miracles and moments of revelation that we have had. We can't forget these past events and experiences in order to set our eyes on the future. We need to take these memories with us as fuel for the journey.

God has designed it so that as we remember and think about all these miracles and answers to prayer, faith rises up in us which enables us to fight and overcome difficulties in the present! That's why so many of the men of God who wrote prayers in the Bible start praying by listing off all the miracles which happened in the generations before them as a testament to His goodness and mercy. In the Psalms we see a common theme about remembering God's power and goodness:

> '*In You our fathers trusted; they trusted You and You delivered them. To You they cried out and they were delivered; in You they trusted and were not disappointed.*' **(Psalm 22:4-5)**

In the Old Testament, the people of God carried around the ark of the covenant. It was an ornately decorated box which symbolised and carried the presence of God. Only the priests were allowed to carry the precious box when it wasn't in the tabernacle. Inside it were reminders of some of the major miracles that had happened on the travels of the Israelites. There were the tablets which had the 10 commandments written on them, a portion of manna to remind them of the miraculous provision of food for them in the desert and there was Aaron's rod that had budded miraculously to remind them of God's power in the plagues. These are all great stories, which you can read about in the book of Exodus and Numbers 17.

The key thing is that God organised it so that everywhere the people went they had reminders of times when He showed up in miraculous ways.

My family has a huge glass vase, which sits in a significant place on our kitchen windowsill. It is there as our thanksgiving vase where we regularly put little pebbles in, on which we write our thanks to God for answers to prayer and miracles. It's the closest thing we can do to demonstrate that we want to always remember those small and big miracles. It's easier than building large stone memorials like they did in the Old Testament. We want to be people who are constantly meditating on past stories of God's goodness and our own experiences so that our faith will be built consistently stronger.

So it is very much a journey of forgetting the past, being responsible for how we respond to the past and meditating on the past so that we become whole.

**A question and some Bible verses to study:**
Question: How can we get the balance between meditating on the past, dealing with the past and forgetting the past?

> '... Take a jar and put an omerful of manna in it before the Lord to be kept throughout your generations. As the Lord commanded Moses, so Aaron placed it before The Testimony to be kept.' **(Exodus 16:33-34)**

> I shall remember the deeds of the Lord, surely I will remember your wonders of old.' **(Psalm 119:24)**

> 'I shall remember the deeds of the Lord, surely I will remember your wonders of old. I will meditate on all your work and muse on Your deeds. Your way O God is holy, what God is great like our God?' **(Psalm 77:11-13)**

> 'Surely you desire truth in the inner parts; you teach me wisdom in the inmost place. Cleanse me with hyssop, and I will be clean; wash me, and I will be whiter than snow.' **(Psalm 51:6-7)**

> 'Do not call to mind the former things, or ponder the things of the past. Behold I will do something new, now it will spring forth; will you be aware of it? I will make a roadway in the wilderness, rivers in the desert...'
> **(Isaiah 43:18-19)**

> 'The Lords loving kindness indeed never cease, for His compassions never fail. They are new every morning; great is Your faithfulness.'
> **(Lamentations 3:23)**

> 'Brethren I do not regard myself as having laid hold of it and yet; but one thing I do; forgetting what lies behind and reaching forward to what lies ahead. I press on toward the goal for the prize of the upward call of God in Christ Jesus.' **(Philippians 3:13-14)**

*'So then, my beloved, just as you have always obeyed, not as in my presence only, but now much more in my absence, work out your salvation with fear and trembling.'* **(Philippians 2:12)**

*'Therefore if anyone is in Christ, he is a new creature; the old things passed away; behold, new things have come.'* **(2 Corinthians 5:17)**

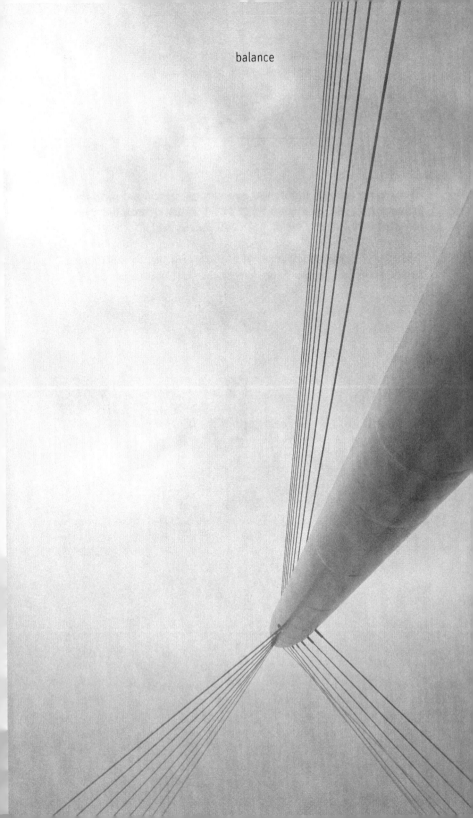

balance

# Chapter 5

## A positive culture and an honest culture

We are so blessed to know Jesus and have a hope and a future because of His grace and mercy to us. We are urged throughout the Bible to remain thankful at all times, to think about God's goodness to us and speak about it as much as possible.

We are also warned about the detriments of being grumbling, unthankful people. The story of the Israelites spending 40 years camped in the wilderness is a tale of people who complained almost continually. Moses was led to despair as he tried to encourage them to remain thankful after yet another miraculous provision or miracle.

> 'So the people grumbled at Moses saying, 'what shall we eat?'
> **(Exodus 16:2)**

Food was provided and yet a short time later,

> 'the people quarrelled with Moses and said, "Give us water that we might drink." And Moses said to them, "Why do you quarrel with me? Why do you test the Lord?"' **(Exodus 17:1-2)**

When we see these attitudes it makes sense why, in the initial exit from Egypt, God instructed the people to remain silent while Moses had to hold his staff and hand above the waters to see them parted in order for them to escape the army. It wouldn't have been easy moving all those people through the Red Sea while they fought and grumbled!

### The power of words
The first words that are spoken in the Bible are words for creation. God made the world by his words. Our words have creative power too because we are made in the image of God. Words were not designed primarily for

communication but to create our own world. Therefore it is vital to speak positive words that build and don't destroy. Grumbling and complaining bring negativity to our lives. They lock us into a state of sadness that God wants to see us free from. Our words are like keys.

In the book of Luke we read the story of John the Baptist. His father Zacharias was told about the baby's imminent arrival by an angel. Zacharias was not convinced and said to the angel, 'How will I know this for certain?' (Luke 1:18) This question demonstrated his lack of faith and so he was told that he would be unable to speak until the baby was born. God needed to ensure that this miracle wasn't going to be destroyed by a man's negative words.

These following Bible verses further help us understand the power of our words.

'Life and death are in the power of the tongue...'
**(Proverbs 18:21)**

'Kind words heal and help, cutting words wound and maim.'
**(Proverbs 15:4)**

'The mouth of the righteous is a fountain of life...'
**(Proverbs 10:11)**

We can see through these verses and stories the importance of speaking positive words to create blessing and favour and the value of not grumbling or complaining. However, we need to ensure honesty and not pretence!

### The need to remain transparent and honest
When things are going great it's easy to be thankful and feel deep gratitude. Sometimes, however, life can be continuously hard and it's in these times it's more difficult to stay positive. We need to seek to speak positive words over our lives and the lives of others whilst we remain honest about our struggles. If we become people who only speak positive words and bottle up all the negative thoughts and emotions in order to stay controlled and cheerful, we have misunderstood the principle of transparency.

We are told in Matthew 5:8 that those who are pure in heart will see

God. The word 'pure' in Greek actually means 'transparent' and so we can get a glimpse of the value of honesty and transparency. We need to be honest about how hard it can be to live in this world as a follower of Jesus. We are blessed and favoured but also persecuted and ostracised. It's almost impossible to have real relationships with people who are pretending that everything is great, while harbouring pain and hurt. Honesty builds and protects relationships.

> *'If we say that we have fellowship with Him and yet walk in the darkness, we lie and do not practise the truth but if we walk in the light as He himself is in the light we have fellowship with each other and the blood of Jesus his Son cleanses us from all sin.'* **(1 John 1: 6-7)**

The Psalms of David are expressions of a man who was chased, hid in caves and had a lot of trials but was confident in communicating them to God in prayer. He didn't use polite positive words but spoke the truth from his heart. He made some shockingly emotive expressions of his anger, frustration and hurt as he faced persecution and difficulties. He did, however, always remind himself of past evidence of Gods goodness, he talked of the importance of dwelling on His faithfulness and staying close to Him as he prayed, to keep his attitude on track.

**Being an aroma of life and death**

We are not usually chased like David but we do often face problems, trials and difficulties. Just by being followers of Jesus we can be misunderstood by the people around us, as we often have to live our lives opposed to the culture of this land. As we try to *'honour others above ourselves'* (Romans 12:10) rather than focus on our own needs, we can be seen as odd. We are to be in the world but not of it.

> *'If you were of the world, the world would love its own; but because you are not of the world, but I chose you out of the world, because of this the world hates you.'* **(John 15: 19)**

It's normal to feel a degree of discomfort being here on earth as we become increasingly aware of our desire for Him and His Kingdom's reign.

People can often treat us with confusion and dislike. Soon after moving to Bath to start the church I was at a dinner party. I was chatting to another mum and after several hours of chat and laughter she asked me what I did. When I replied, she got up from the table, looked horrified and said loudly, 'I would never have sat next to you had I known. That's awful. I don't want to talk to you ever again.' She didn't talk to me despite my efforts for about two years! Now she speaks to me happily with the other mums, but it took her two years of watching me from a distance!

We are the aroma of death and the aroma of life (2 Corinthians 2:15-16). We scare some people because we remind them of the big questions in life they often want to forget. We don't completely fit in because there are vast differences when living a life focused on pleasing God rather than merely pleasing man. We need to be honest about our feelings and struggles whilst not complaining and grumbling. We can find encouragement from each other and find healing in the presence of Jesus.

### Sing O Barren

There is something profound about Isaiah 54:1, 'sing O barren woman, she who has no child, sing.' This verse helps us begin to understand the power of singing, praising and declaring truth in the midst of our tough times. Our barrenness is about any area of our life where we desire and long for growth, solution, or an answer. We could be living life aware of a lack in an area of our lives, or desperately in need of a solution to a problem. It could be that we are financially barren, relationally barren or spiritually dry and barren. We are told to sing in the midst of our barrenness, not when we get through to the time of answer and solution, but right in the middle while it's still dark, dry and empty. God knows that declaring His goodness in the midst of the difficulty brings a release of faith and hope which can keep us walking through the valley.

The verse continues with an encouragement to expand and enlarge. How many people in the midst of their emptiness want to build extra rooms on their house to contain the overflow? Yet this is our instruction. We need to sing and then get busy, with an expectancy of seeing God move and bring solution. God responds to faith. We are told that faith pleases God, (Hebrews 11:6) so that has to be a good thing!

In our family, we felt that God had asked us to expand last year and so we started looking for new houses. We meanwhile bought a new sofa ready for the move, which has made the waiting harder than it would have been had we not acted, but we wanted to show God we believed Him and we were ready. Enlargement isn't usually literal, but in this case we knew it was, so we took small steps of faith along the way, which were important ones for us as a family, to raise faith and hope for our new season.

### Honest and edifying

So how can we facilitate a church where we can be honest and yet remember, and not dilute, the understanding of the power of words? I want people who are hurting and needy to be able to express that in church and not be judged or lectured. I want people to be able to pour out their hearts to God about the pain that they feel without them feeling that maybe they are losing their salvation. Life can be tough and we need safe churches where real stories are shared and mess is welcomed.

I once taught on this subject at church and a student came up to me at the end and said she was relieved that she could now tell me that she didn't like me. I was surprised and didn't have the chance, due to my shock, to explain that honesty doesn't give us liberty to hurt each other.

So let's try and create a culture where we can be honest; our strong, difficult feelings are not rejected; we commit to praising God in every circumstance and we don't judge others who are struggling. We need to remain thankful people who don't grumble and complain whilst being honest and transparent about our struggles and feelings because we are not meant to feel completely at home here on earth. Let us remember that for some people, life is harder than others so we mustn't boss others around but gently encourage them, whilst remembering that we are not in their shoes.

### A question and some Bible verses to study:

Question: How can we be honest, truthful and real but also use our words to create our world and edify each other?

*'Life and death are in the power of the tongue...'* (**Proverbs 18:21**)

'For we are a fragrance of Christ to God among those who are being saved and among those who are perishing; to the one an aroma of death to death, to the other an aroma from life to life.' **(2 Corinthians 2:15-16)**

'For our citizenship is in heaven...' **(Philippians 3:20)**

'So then you are no longer strangers and aliens but you are fellow citizens with the saints and are of God's household.' **(Ephesians 2:19)**

'Kind words heal and help, cutting words wound and maim.' **(Proverbs 15:4)**

'The mouth of the righteous is a fountain of life...' **(Proverbs 10:11)**

'If we say that we have fellowship with Him and yet walk in the darkness, we lie and do not practise the truth but if we walk in the light as He himself is in the light we have fellowship with each other and the blood of Jesus his Son cleanses us from all sin.' **(1 John 1:6-7)**

'Therefore encourage one another and build up one another, just as you also are doing.' **(1 Thessalonians 5:11)**

'So then we pursue the things which make for peace and the building up of one another.' **(Romans 14:19)**

'Let no corrupting talk come out of your mouths, but only such as is good for building up, as fits the occasion, that it may give grace to those who hear.' **(Ephesians 4:29)**

'Iron sharpens iron, and one man sharpens another.' **(Proverbs 27:17)**

'Preach the word; be ready in season and out of season; reprove, rebuke, and exhort, with complete patience and teaching.' **(2 Timothy 4:2)**

balance

chapter 6 - everything is possible for God
so does that mean that we do nothing?

51

# Chapter 6

## Everything is possible for God
## so does that mean that we do nothing?

**Nothing is impossible for God (Luke 1:37)**
We love to sing this verse and declare it over our own lives as a fantastic truth that makes faith rise and excitement build while we think of all the answers to prayer that we need. Many different times in my life, when things were going wrong and I needed a miracle, I've had to really *know* this verse is true; God really can do the impossible. I said it, I believed it and God has often done what He loves to do; miracles. As we give our lives to follow the God of Abraham, Isaac and Jacob, we need to practice dwelling on all the stories of God doing the impossible.

I look back at the amount of times we have employed a new staff member for the church offices when there wasn't any spare money. We had to believe that God would provide and He did; I know God is the God of the impossible.

When we have prayed for people and seen them totally healed and restored, when doctors have said they would die; I know that God is the God of the impossible.

When I have seen babies in the womb who were diagnosed with problems, born totally well and whole; I know that God is the God of the impossible.

When we as a church bought a tired old building that had been left unused for several years, renovated it and used it for four years and then made huge amounts of money on it; I know our God is the God of the impossible.

When we have prayed for couples who had struggled for years and it seemed their marriage was falling apart, whilst the situation looked so unhopeful, we have seen hope restored and healing happen; we know our God is the God who does the impossible.

When I faced malaria and many other close encounters with death,

I cried out to God knowing he is able to do abundantly more than we can ask or imagine. I whispered that I know in all things God can do the impossible and I have survived.

I can tell you my God is the God of miracles. You can say they are coincidences, but all I'd say is that they keep happening every time we pray. He can go beyond our expectations, more than we could possibly ask, yet sometimes He is silent and our prayers do not seem to have been heard. Even in times where He seems silent and far away, the darkness will end and our faith will be strengthened as we praise Him and trust Him to do the impossible. Nothing is too hard for Him and His love for us is unique and perfect.

### What does God expect us to do if He can do everything?
So when we are in relationship with such an awesome God whose love and power is so vast, what role do we have? Do we just wait for Him to 'do His God thing'?

In the story of creation in (Genesis 1 - 2) we see that God did the impossible by creating something out of nothing, then asked human kind to have an active role in stewarding His creation. Partnership and co-labouring is birthed.

There are many stories of partnership and co-labouring in the Old Testament that are particularly encouraging in times of difficulty. At the time when the Israelites were just escaping from Egypt but were terrified of being chased Moses said to the people, *'Do not fear! Stand by and see the salvation of the Lord which He will accomplish for you today. The Lord will fight for you while you keep silent'* (Exodus 14:16-21). So here we see God destroying the army that is coming to kill them. He destroyed them because the people obeyed His instructions and so worked in partnership with Him. We see Moses being asked to hold a staff up as he stretched out his hand over the sea as a practical act of faith. The people were asked to remain silent so that their words wouldn't cause destruction. God did the miracle but the people had to do something that didn't feel natural or sensible to them in a time of crisis.

God wants to heal people but He asks that we lay hands on them. God wants us to have healthy relationships and so He has given us the Bible that is packed full of wisdom and good and bad examples of friendships

chapter 6 - everything is possible for God
so does that mean that we do nothing?

53

and family life. God wants us to know peace so He tells us that '*as you draw near to God, He will draw near to you*' (James 4: 7-9). His presence brings peace because He is the prince of peace. We were not designed to know peace outside His presence. He gives us lots of instructions of what we do to co-labour with Him. Without Him we can do nothing of worth but with Him we can do the impossible.

In the book of James we see a whole flow of partnership examples. James 5:13 looks at the problem of sickness and the appropriate response was a typical partnership between people and God. If the leaders anoint with oil and pray, God will heal. In verse 17 we see Elijah praying for drought and then rain. He prayed and God did the miracle. God is looking for people who will move so He can do extraordinary things.

**With provision**

In Psalm 35:27 we read that '*The Lord takes delight in the prosperity of His people.*' So in context to this verse it's worth studying to find out how this prosperity is meant to arrive in the lives of the people of God.

Let's look at two verses to start with. '*My God will supply all your needs according to His riches in glory in Christ Jesus*'. (Philippians 4:15-19) This seems to partner with the other verse, '*it is He who is giving you the power to make wealth*' (Deuteronomy 8:18). The verse in Philippians could be read as permission to remain passive and expectant but it was written in the context of the people of Philippi who were being demonstratively generous. Also, the Deuteronomy verse seems to be indicating that we are required to be active in creating wealth, and grateful for God's guidance, strength and creative power in steering us to do so. When these verses are taken out of context, it can appear to us that we do nothing but wait for God. Sometimes, God does tell us to wait, but even then we are either to stand, which denotes a position of expectancy, or we are told to wait on Him in faith. There is always something that we do to partner with God when bringing His reign onto earth. Let's look at some of the context of the verse in Phillipians:

> '*You yourselves also know, Philippians, that at the first preaching of the gospel, after I left Macedonia, no church shared with me in the matter of giving and receiving but you alone; for even in Thessalonica*

*you sent a gift more than once for my needs. Not that I seek the gift itself, but I seek for the profit which increases to your account. But I have received everything in full and have an abundance; I am amply supplied, having received from Epaphroditus what you have sent, a fragrant aroma, an acceptable sacrifice, well-pleasing to God. And my God will supply all your needs according to His riches in glory in Christ Jesus.'* **(Philippians 4:15-19)**

### Being in partnership with the King of Kings

It's easy to dream dreams and wait expectantly for God to move but that is not how we were created to live. God designed us to work hard and enjoy the fruit of our labour. We read in Ecclesiastes 5:3 that *'the dream comes through much effort'*, and I certainly know that this is true. When the dream comes from God, there is an ease and liberty in it that helps to confirm His will, yet hard work, grit and determination are still required.

God has equipped us with everything we need to live a life pleasing to Him. He has planned good works for us to do:

*'For we are His workmanship, created in Christ Jesus for good works, which God has prepared beforehand so we could walk in them.'* **(Ephesians 2:10)**

*He delights to work with us to see people experience His love, power, mercy, presence and healing, 'For we are God's fellow workers.'* **(1 Corinthians 3:9)**

*Paul continually expressed that all the successes he experienced were due to the grace of God. He repeats throughout his letters his dependence on God and the delight of partnering with Him. 'Most gladly I will boast about my weaknesses, so that the power of Christ may dwell in me...For when I am weak, then I am strong.'* **(2 Corinthians 12:9-10)**

Even Jesus said that He only does what He sees His Father God do. This shows the ultimate partnership experience and models how we are meant to submit to Him. We have to still our hearts and choose to listen to the

chapter 6 - everything is possible for God
so does that mean that we do nothing?

55

still small voice of the Holy Spirit, directing us in our lives to do all that He desires for us to accomplish.

Look what Jesus says in answer to the question of His role:
*'Therefore Jesus was saying to them, "Truly truly, I say to you, the son of man can do nothing of Himself, unless it is something he sees the Father doing; for whatever the father does, these things the son also does in like manner."* **(John 5:19)**

*'...No one could do these signs that You do unless God is with Him'.* **(John 3:2)**

### If you... then I will...
This seems to be a theme throughout the Old Testament as we read the many promises of God for those who obeyed and followed His instructions. Deuteronomy 28 is a pinnacle of these relationship guidelines because the promises of blessings are extraordinarily expressed and the same line is repeated throughout; *'if you diligently obey the Lord your God, being careful to do all His commandments... then I will...'* (Deuteronomy 28:1)

We were designed to partner together with God for whom nothing is impossible!

God loves to do the impossible and He loves to co-labour with us as we do that which is possible. We read how this partnership works in Ephesians 3:20, *'Now to Him who is able to do far more abundantly beyond all that we ask or think, according to the power that is at work within us'.* We become excited about all that God is going to do, which is beyond our wildest dreams. Then the verse ends by reminding us that we are containers of His power and therefore can do all that He does. We don't just get to sit back, relax and see Him do amazing works without us co-operating. We are only limited by our own desire to work with Him in partnership to bring heaven onto earth. The Bible tells us in Luke 1:37 that *'nothing will be impossible with God'* whilst we are encouraged to follow the apostle Paul and say that *'I can do all things through Christ who strengthens me.'* (Philippians 4:13) The two verses compliment each other and help us to begin to understand God's expectation of us as His children.

What an amazing thing to ponder on; that God would choose to co-labour with us to extend His Kingdom on earth, and have works planned specifically for us before the creation of the world.


**A question and some Bible verses to study:**
Question: If God can do everything and nothing is impossible for Him, what is my role and how do I know when to act or speak and when to stand or stay silent while He moves?

> *"When I shut up the heavens so that there is no rain, or command locusts to devour the land or send a plague among my people, if my people, who are called by my name, will humble themselves and pray and seek my face and turn from their wicked ways, then I will hear from heaven, and I will forgive their sin and will heal their land.'*
> **(2 Chronicles 7:13-14 New International version)**

> *'Submit yourselves, then, to God. Resist the devil, and he will flee from you. Come near to God and he will come near to you...'* **(James 4:7-8)**

> *'But Jesus beheld them, and said to them, with men this is impossible; but with God all things are possible.'* **(Matthew 19:26)**

> *'... Truly, truly, I say to you, the son of man can do nothing of Himself, unless it is something he sees the Father doing; for whatever the father does, these things the son also does in like manner.'* **(John 5:19)**

> *'...No one could do these signs that You do unless God is with Him'.*
> **(John 3:2)**

> *'Truly, truly, I say to you, he who believes in Me, the works that I do, he will do also; and greater works than these he will do ; because I go to the Father. Whatever you ask in My name, that will I do, so that the Father may be glorified in the Son. If you ask Me anything in My name, I will do it.'*
> **(John 14:12-14)**

'*Therefore, take up the full armor of God, so that you will be able to resist in the evil day, and having done everything, to stand firm. Stand firm therefore…*' **(Ephesians 6:13-14)**

'*What use is it, my brethren, if someone says he has faith but he has no works? Can that faith save him? If a brother or sister is without clothing and in need of daily food, and one of you says to them, "Go in peace, be warmed and be filled," and yet you do not give them what is necessary for their body, what use is that? Even so faith, if it has no works, is dead, being by itself.*'
**(James 2:14-17)**

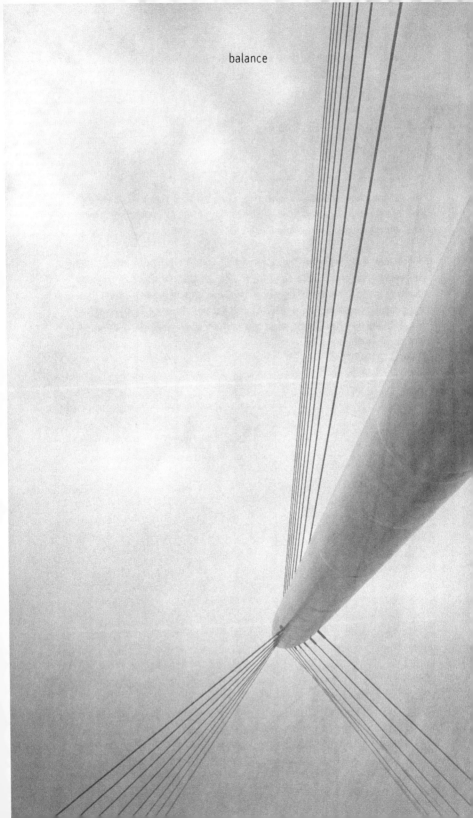
balance

# Chapter 7

# The natural and the spiritual

When I was an intensely spiritual teenager, I was greatly helped by a teacher who noticed my enthusiasm for all things Bible related. She took me aside and whispered a common saying; 'don't be so heavenly minded that you are no earthly good.' This is a useful tip to use when we try to balance our life on Earth with our hearts in heaven, aware of the heavenly dimension but with our feet firmly placed on the ground. We are living as followers of Jesus on this earth with real bodies, real needs and responsibilities. Yet the reality of the unseen spiritual realm is as real as the chairs we are sitting on now. This is something that we in the West are usually less familiar with than people who grow up in regions such as Africa, where the spiritual realm is spoken of naturally.

### The spiritual realm

When the spiritual realm is accepted as real, it opens a new perspective in life which science is unable to fully comprehend. The spiritual realm is unseen and unquantifiable which leads many people to choose to either ignore it or just try to solve any perceived mysteries with rational arguments. It seems ironic that many people who don't follow Jesus believe in the spiritual realm being a place of some kind of power and mystery, yet many who choose to follow Jesus don't really believe.

Since God is unseen, it seems to be important for followers of Jesus to believe in an entire unseen spiritual realm. The books of Revelation and Daniel in the Bible help us to grasp some of the breadth of the spiritual world that we are not usually visually exposed to. The stories in these books are there to help us widen our small thinking and help us understand that there is more than we can see with our natural eyes.

The books and subsequent films by CS Lewis about Narnia as a magical land running parallel to our own, can also be helpful in stimulating our imaginations to understand the warfare that is constantly surrounding us.

Many people grow up familiar with the cartoon of a devil on one shoulder tempting and whispering evil, and an angel on the other shoulder suggesting good. It's not an illustration that is too far from reality. Paul the apostle speaks boldly of his experience with the spiritual world that seeks to create division and deception.

> *'For our struggle is not against flesh and blood but against the rulers, against the powers, against the world forces of the darkness, against the spiritual forces of wickedness in the heavenly places.'*
> **(Ephesians 6:12)**

In relating to and understanding an unseen world, we need faith. In Hebrews 11 we read of the centrality of faith in order to hold onto that *'which is hoped for and not yet seen'*. Faith is an expression of our individual trust in that which is unseen. There seems to be an acceptance that we as followers of Jesus need faith to believe in an invisible God, but there is less enthusiasm to believe in other unseen realities that are supernatural. Most believers are comfortable with the supernatural element being a simple prayer for others resulting in healing and freedom, but that's where it often stops.

We are also taught in Hebrews 11 about the power of the unseen, but often Western churches seem to reframe that to fit their own personal experiences in order to feel safe and comfortable. We need to be reminded that *'by faith we understand that the worlds were prepared by the word of God, so that what is seen was not made out of things which are visible.'* (Hebrews 11:3)

The Bible teaches that we have an unseen enemy who seeks to destroy us (John 10:10) and that this enemy loves it when we limit our view of the world according to what we have experienced and seen with our natural eyes. It means that we are not much of a threat to his strategy to destroy the plans that God has for us. If we don't understand how the enemy works, or if we don't acknowledge his existence or purpose, it's pretty hard for us to be able to know how to deal with his attacks and plans to harm us. God will tell us whatever we need to know to bring His rule into situations. These directional whispers are often not heard by those who actually believe that the supernatural enemy action that they may hear about is exaggerated fiction. It's helpful to live on this earth as people who generally accept that many questions about the unseen will only be answered fully in eternity when we are face to face with Jesus. While we reside here, He wants to reveal answers to some mysteries as we seek Him. He is looking for people to hear Him and reveal these kingdom keys of freedom to unlock the broken, hurting and confused.

*'Call to me and I will answer you and I will tell you great and mighty things that you do not know.'* **(Jeremiah 33:3)**

**Taking responsibility**
We must take responsibility ourselves to keep our eyes are fixed on Jesus, as we seek Him and His kingdom first. We must never forget that we are in a spiritual battle so that we are not distracted by temptation or superficiality, but determined to keep our eyes focused on the eternal perspective.

*'But there's more to life for us. We're citizens of high heaven! We're waiting the arrival of the saviour, the master, Jesus Christ who will transform our earthly bodies into glorious bodies like his very own.'*
**(Philippians 3:20 The Message)**

Our thoughts about the unseen world need to be balanced with our thinking about the natural world so that we live life wisely. Some people speak of experiencing 'the enemy's attack' when they face temptation over choices, and although this can be the case, (Matthew 4:9-11) the enemy doesn't usually need to help us with distractions and temptations because we as humans, seem quite capable of providing enough of these ourselves. So whilst the enemy does plan to hurt us, we cannot blame him for everything that goes wrong, because there could be a host of reasons for our trials and temptations.

**Spiritual laws**
We live in a society that seems to grasp that there are laws to try and protect the people. As a norm, people understand speed limits, sign posts, paying taxes, what is acceptable behaviour and the consequences of not

abiding by these rules. There are also spiritual laws that make little sense to the natural mind yet hold enormous power. For example, the Kingdom principles of reverence for the presence of the Holy Spirit, the principles of sowing and reaping, of honouring others, of the first becoming last and the last first, tithing, the importance of the communion and baptism. Many of these spiritual laws confuse people who don't follow Jesus because of their desire to comprehend everything with reasoning. Yet when we honour the spiritual laws, we are exercising faith in the unseen, which honours God.

We are told in Colossians 3:2 to *'Set our mind on things above not on earthly things'* and when we live as followers of Jesus our lives are able to flow with faith, not just for ourselves but for all that God wants to release in the world. We are here for such a time as this to accomplish assignments that God has planned for us before the beginning of time. We need to follow the spiritual laws to ensure that we are being the best that we can be.

**Taking authority: The power of the blood of Jesus**
One of the most central spiritual laws that we hold is the power of the blood of Jesus. I preached a series on this last year and it was extraordinary to see the consequences of the power of God bringing freedom and breakthrough. When we speak of the blood of Jesus, with a revelation of the power of His blood, we tap into a spiritual law that is understood in the unseen realm more than here on earth. As we pray in faith, standing on the truth that the blood of Jesus has washed us as white as snow and has made a way for us to be in relationship with God, the creator, the saviour, the healer and the almighty, we walk in a new boldness. When we break bread and take communion, we are partaking in a symbol that represents the power of the blood of Jesus to make a way for us to live. It has defeated the power of death and sin, cleansed us and made us right before God, restored us and broken every power against us. The blood of Jesus has delivered us from the dominion of darkness into the kingdom of God and has set our feet on a solid rock with a robe of righteousness covering us. The drink that we take, that represents the blood, draws us to a life changing moment where we remember the payment of our salvation and the need for that final, ultimate holy sacrifice of Jesus; to die for our

sins so that we may live. The blood of Jesus represents life, wholeness, freedom, forgiveness and light in the darkness. Yet it is a spiritual law that sounds crazy to the rational mind that tries to comprehend it. When we walk in the revelation of the blood of Jesus we can know the power of God working for us for freedom to set us free. When we ignore the spiritual power of this blood, we deny the full extent of the inheritance that comes from the death of Jesus because the promises can only be received by faith. The blood of Jesus makes demons tremble, strongholds quake and curses set against us come to nothing. The powers of darkness understand the price that was paid by the sinless saviour, on our behalf, to set us free.

## The natural

As we remember the spiritual realm and the unseen battle, we also need to remember that we are not yet residents of heaven but are here as residents of Earth! We can't allow ourselves to spend the short time we have on Earth dreaming of our eternal home but must be focused on the mission that He has given us to accomplish. Each day we are able to do incredible things, that can be a taste of heaven to people, because we bring an atmosphere of hope, love and freedom. We can move mountains, see healing and shift things in the unseen realm by prayer. Every time we obey God's specific instruction to us, whether it is to ring a person that we think of, smile at a passer by, send a text to encourage someone or go out of our way to pray for someone, we are part of God's plan to bring heaven's reign onto this earth.

God desires that our life is filled with action and words that match. James makes it very clear that *'Faith without action is dead'* (James 2:17). We then get told, in 1 John 3:18, that we must love, *'not in word or tongue but in deed and truth'*.

We are not expected to be people who are so heavenly minded that we only dream and pray and wait. We are called to be co-labourers with God and act. It's impossible to steer a ship that is stationary but it is easy when it's moving. God requires us to be people who don't stay stationary but move so that He can continually guide us.

When the prophet Micah asked God what was expected of him, he received a clear response:

*'He has told you oh man what is good; and what does the Lord require of you but to do justice, to love kindness, and to walk humbly with your God.'* **(Micah 6:8)**

God gives us practical instructions about the position of our heart, our behaviour and the use of time, energy and money.

### Common sense
Some of the answers to our problems are practical and demand the use of common sense. Sadly this ability seems seriously less than common! Proverbs is a book of wisdom in the Bible that is full of practical tips about relationships, finance, attitudes, the use of time and other fundamental areas of life. People who lose perspective about the spiritual and the natural can end up living with disaster that could be avoided. They can end up experiencing problems and pain that had natural, easily avoided causes. We are created to live in community and help each other find wisdom for life from our own experiences of mistakes and successes. God has planted many answers to our issues in the minds and hearts of others around us. I have a picture in my mind that I often use to explain our interdependence, which is about us all creating an invisible jigsaw puzzle. Inside each of us we hold a glass jar of jigsaw puzzle pieces, which others need to help the pictures in their puzzles become clearer. As we journey through life we are able to give people puzzle pieces and receive them from others to help us understand more and more of who God is, His character and our identity and specific callings. God loves to use us as His messengers.

So we need to be people who follow Jesus by understanding that we are part of a spiritual battle, whether we want to be or not. We need to have our eyes fixed on Jesus, our hearts in heaven and use common sense as we live each day trying to obey God's instructions.

**Some questions and some Bible verses to study:**
Question: How do I live with my spiritual senses alert and awakened to the spiritual realm? What spiritual laws do I wrestle with?

*'If I told you earthly things and you do not believe, how will you believe if I tell you heavenly things?'* **(John 3:12)**

*'He has told you, O man, what is good; And what does the LORD require of you but to do justice, to love kindness, And to walk humbly with your God?'* **(Micah 6:8)**

*'Therefore, since we have so great a cloud of witnesses surrounding us, let us also lay aside every encumbrance and the sin which so easily entangles us, and let us run with endurance the race that is set before us, fixing our eyes on Jesus, the author and perfecter of faith, who for the joy set before Him endured the cross, despising the shame, and has sat down at the right hand of the throne of God.'* **(Hebrews 12:1-2).**

*'Be of sober spirit, be on the alert. Your adversary, the devil, prowls around like a roaring lion, seeking someone to devour.'* **(1 Peter 5:8)**

*'In the same way, prayer is essential in this on going warfare. Pray hard and long. Pray for your brothers and sisters. Keep your eyes open. Keep each other's spirits up so that no one falls behind or drops out.'* **(Ephesians 6:18 The Message)**

*'For the wages of sin is death, but the free gift of God is eternal life in Christ Jesus our Lord.'* **(Romans 6:23)**

*'And they overcame him because of the blood of the Lamb and because of the word of their testimony, and they did not love their life even when faced with death.'* **(Revelation 12:11)**

*'Do not be deceived, God is not mocked; for whatever a man sows, this he will also reap.'* **(Galatians 6:7)**

*'...If we walk in the Light as He Himself is in the Light, we have fellowship with one another, and the blood of Jesus His Son cleanses us from all sin.'* **(1 John 1:7)**

*'Therefore, brethren, since we have confidence to enter the holy place by the blood of Jesus.'* **(Hebrews 10:19)**

*'But now in Christ Jesus you who formerly were far off have been brought near by the blood of Christ.'* **(Ephesians 2:13)**

**Daniel 10: 1-21 Daniel Is Terrified by a Vision**

balance

# Chapter 8

## Grace, Mercy and Justice

The words 'grace' and 'mercy' are bursting with meaning and are central values to the follower of Jesus. These words express the wonder of being forgiven, loved, restored and cherished by God himself and our response is naturally one of deep gratitude and thankfulness. As churches we sing and teach consistently about love, grace and mercy. It's the foundation of our salvation. We love Jesus because He first loved us. We are adopted into His family as we choose to give the leadership of our lives to Him. As we choose to follow Him we are reliant on His love and His mercy towards us.

We seem to sing and talk less about justice here in the West, yet we know that the foundation of the throne of God is built on righteousness and justice. (Psalm 89:14) In Micah 6:8 we are given an idea of what is important to God:

> 'He has told you, O man, what is good; And what does the LORD require of you But to do justice, to love kindness, And to walk humbly with your God?'

I reckon it's important for us to think, wrestle and discuss the balance of mercy, grace and justice as we try and work out the reality of how we're meant to think, react, pray and live as followers of Jesus wanting to glorify God in our lives.

### Love

1 Corinthians 13 is a well known chapter which describes love in a detailed way. It is often read at weddings as people start out on a journey of commitment to love each other above themselves. The verses actually describe Jesus and His character and therefore are a description of how we are meant to live as God transforms us from the inside to become like Jesus.

The thing that we find hard to grasp with the limitations of language is that God is love. We hear of His love and assume that He is loving like our grandma or our best friend. It is easy to forget that He is the very source of and personification of love. He can't be unloving, have a bad day or be less than fully Love. In our society love often seems to be portrayed as a feeling that changes all the time or is earned by behavior, and this is not like the love of God. Love can be seen as cheap, because the media portrays people falling in love and then losing that love the next day and this also makes it hard to understand the real depth of love that God is. God's love never changes, is constant and faithful. The depth of His love for us is mind blowing as we remember that He planned for us and knows us deeply. As we grasp His love, it melts and transforms our hearts and lives. He is a God who dances about us and rejoices over us.

> 'The Lord your God is in your midst, a victorious warrior. He will exalt over you with joy, He will quiet you with his love, He will rejoice over you with shouts of joy.' **(Zephaniah 3:17)**

> 'The one who does not love does not know God for God is love.' **(1 John 4:8)**

**Grace is God's empowerment.**

> '...My grace is sufficient for you, for my power is made perfect in weakness...' **(2 Corinthians 12:9)**

Paul the apostle had to deal with some people's misconceptions about the concept of grace. (Romans 6:1-3) The same misconceptions seem to be prevalent now, as people like to take the word to mean we can do as we wish, because God forgives us anyway. I don't think so! The word grace does not mean love that excuses us, as many seem to believe, it means a loving gift of power to live a life of obedience. 'Charis' is the predominant word for 'grace' in Greek and 'charisma' is the specific gift. Grace is the empowerment of God that allows us to go beyond our natural ability. It is an extravagant gift to equip and help us. Maybe we should try substituting the word 'empowerment' every time we read the word grace in the New Testament because that will show us that grace really is.

**Mercy**

Mercy is defined as the benevolent forgiveness of God when punishment is deserved. It is also described as a compassionate response. In Luke 10:30-37 we read the story of the Good Samaritan which Jesus tells to the crowds in order to answer the question, 'who is my neighbour?' The story gives examples of different people's responses to a man in tragic circumstances. The story is named in the modern Bible after the Samaritan man who responded to the stranger in compassionate, generous and extravagant ways. Jesus draws the conclusion,

> 'Which of these three do you think proved to be a neighbour to the man who fell into the robbers' hands?" And he said, "The one who showed mercy toward him." Then Jesus said to him, "Go and do the same." ' **(Luke 10: 37)**

Jesus explains that we should all be people who react with mercy and compassion towards others.

**The conflict between mercy and justice**

Justice is defined as the administering of deserved punishment or reward. Sometimes I struggle, while working on the frontlines with broken and damaged people, to know how to seek justice, yet also remain loving, kind and merciful. It only seems possible if I stay humbly walking with God, because justice and mercy sometimes seem in conflict.

The place I see this conflict the most is probably in my work around the criminal justice system. We have always enjoyed visiting and praying for people in prisons and we have taught our teams over the years that we should have mercy regardless of the person or their past. We have also taught that people have to pay the consequences of actions that are against the law of the land. As we continue to be a church who both visit people in prisons, pray for them, love them and tell them about God's love, we are also actively involved in helping people speak up against injustice and we support children, young people and adults as they give evidence in courts about abuse. So we help justice prevail by supporting the process of people being sent to prison as a punishment for their wrong doings, and we demonstrate kindness and mercy by visiting them in prison!

The verse in Micah suddenly becomes an essential piece of wisdom when we looking for clarity about the balance of mercy and justice because as followers of Jesus, to understand how to navigate the right response in difficult situations is impossible unless we are walking humbly with our God.

> 'He has shown you, O man, what is good; and what does the Lord require of you but to do justice, to love kindness and to walk humbly with your God.' **(Micah 6:8)**

When we recognize that there are no formulas but that if we stay in a teachable relationship with God, without pride blinding us, He will show us when to pursue justice (deserved punishment) alongside mercy (forgiveness when punishment is deserved).

### The gospel of nice
A while ago I realized that deep down I had also subconsciously believed that Jesus was always 'nice' and I had to be too. I realized that I had only wrestled with the issues around justice and mercy in relation to global problems and hadn't noticed that I believed the 'western gospel of niceness.' It became clear when we started talking about justice in less obvious global issues, there was aversion from religious people. This was like hitting a cultural wall of niceness, which couldn't tolerate the concept of justice in the local, daily context. The reality that holiness demands justice seems alien to most cultural christians. People are encouraged to speak passionately about justice in the context of sex trafficking or other clearly defined issues, but it seems rare to also grasp the importance of justice in daily life. Justice is essential and fighting for justice needs to be a healthy part of our lives as followers of Jesus. It is more of a central aspect of following Jesus than is currently taught and understood.

> 'Righteousness and justice are the foundation of Your throne; Loving-kindness and truth go before You.' **(Psalm 89:14)**
> **(Also see Psalm 97:2)**

It can be confusing for those of us who are trying to follow Jesus when we hear teaching that is purely on grace, mercy, and the father heart of God without the balance of justice too. It sounds again like a gospel of niceness, which is far removed from the Jesus of the Bible who was far from nice. For many people there doesn't seem to be a healthy Biblical balance in the understanding of the relationship between the Kingdom values of justice, love and mercy.

When working with victims of trauma I often find myself caught in powerful conflicting emotions. When I am working with the victims or survivors of disaster, I am more than extremely aware of their pain, anguish, terror, fear, and exhaustion because they have to cope with their world having been torn apart by someone else's wrongdoing and dysfunction. I guess that the tough thing about being a pastor and a therapist is that I don't see anyone as completely bad, or totally beyond healing. Every perpetrator who has devastated the lives of these vulnerable beautiful people that I work with, was probably abused, hurt and mistreated themselves as a child. They probably didn't have God in their world or a centre to go to where they could process their negative and painful feelings, so I naturally feel mercy toward them. It seems that we need to pursue justice and mercy together. One without the other is going to be imbalanced because God is the God of justice as well as mercy. It's important to see traffickers behind bars and we celebrate when we see victory for our clients when their courage leads to justice and therefore protection of others from the possibility of abuse.

Let's look at how love and mercy can conflict with justice in some example situations. In your children's or a friend's school you find out that a parent has been abusing the children who go round to his house for tea. Is this a time for justice or forgiving, forgetting and mercy?

How about a situation with a work colleague who you find out has been lying about you and causing others to avoid you. They make life really difficult and your boss asks why you aren't as happy as you were. Is this a chance for justice or is it an opportunity to show mercy?

I guess that's the thing: we don't know the answers. There is no formula; no black and white definitive answers. We need to keep walking with God, dependent on His lead and listening to His voice.

**Can I do anything in a world of injustice, and will my love and mercy make any difference?**
When looking at the statistics of injustice in our world and therefore the pain that this causes so many millions of people, it's hard not to feel a mix of strong emotions.

I have two strong images when I reflect on the state of the world today. One is of a mole digging. I have no idea why, but I always find strength in the knowledge that moles spend a lot of time working under the ground, steady and consistent. Only sometimes we get to see something that indicates the productivity of their work. The other is the story of the loaves and the fishes (Luke 9:12-17). I love the fact that whatever we offer to God on the altar of sacrifice, He is able to multiply beyond that which we can imagine. I love the fact that we are not responsible for the breadth of our influence, but we are responsible for the depth.

In 1949 Mother Teresa felt called by God to work with 'the poorest of the poor' in Calcutta, India. She lived a life that demonstrated love, mercy and justice. Despite living a comfortable existence in a convent, she obeyed God and began to serve the poor in India. The first year was especially difficult as she had no income and often had to beg for food and supplies. Despite initial difficulties, Mother Teresa was able to found 'The Missionaries of Charity' in 1950. Its mission was to care for, in her own words, 'the hungry, the naked, the homeless, the crippled, the blind, the lepers, all those people who feel unwanted, unloved, uncared for throughout society, people that have become a burden to the society and are shunned by everyone.' It began with a small group of 13 people. As of 2007, there were 600 missions, schools and shelters in 120 countries.

Whilst it's easy to feel powerless and that we, as a small gathering of people, can make little difference, we can see from this example that when we do what we can from a motive of understanding our mission on this earth, God will multiply our efforts.

We don't have a choice to be impotent and passive. It's not an optional extra to speak on behalf of those who are facing injustice. It's not an optional extra to love people and show mercy. It's integral to being a follower of Jesus. Isaiah states the mission of Jesus and as His followers this has to be our mandate too:

*'The Spirit of God, the Master, is on me because God anointed me. He sent me to preach good news to the poor, heal the heartbroken, announce freedom to all captives, pardon all prisoners. God sent me to announce the year of his grace- a celebration of God's destruction of our enemies- and to comfort all who mourn. To care for the needs of all who mourn in Zion, give them bouquets of roses instead of ashes, messages of joy instead of news of doom, a praising heart instead of a languid spirit. Rename them 'Oaks od Righteousness' planted by God to display his glory. They'll rebuild the old ruins, raise a new city out of the wreckage. They'll start over on the ruined cities, take the rubble left behind and make it new.'*
**(Isaiah 61: 1-7 The Message)**

We have a voice. We can lend it to people and speak up for them and their needs.

We can do and think and act. We are here to do whatever God wants us to do, using our skills, time and money to bring a reign and rule of heaven onto Earth; to bring the Kingdom of God onto Earth and to displace injustice. We bring healing, justice, restoration, love, mercy, grace, kindness and hope.

It's not the media hyped 'you deserve it', perfect, calm lifestyle that comes when living a life of surrender to God's agenda. It is, however, a privileged lifestyle where we co-labour with God and watch while He takes the crumbs of offering and multiplies them to be provision for people who are in need of the good news that Jesus brings.

We can change the statistics.

We can change our communities.

We can love our neighbours and our enemies.

We can bring hope and healing.

We can make a difference.

We can see the tangible extension of God's kingdom here on Earth, as it is in heaven.

**Some questions and some Bible verses to study:**
What can you do today to bring about justice? Where do you feel passionate and where do you feel passive? What's in your hand to use to change situations of injustice?

> 'Then the King will say to those on His right, 'Come, you who are blessed of My Father, inherit the kingdom prepared for you from the foundation of the world. For I was hungry, and you gave Me something to eat; I was thirsty, and you gave Me something to drink; I was a stranger, and you invited Me in; naked, and you clothed Me; I was sick, and you visited Me; I was in prison, and you came to Me.' Then the righteous will answer Him, 'Lord, when did we see You hungry, and feed You, or thirsty, and give You something to drink? And when did we see you a stranger, and invite you in, or naked, and clothe you? When did we see you sick, or in prison, and come to you?' The King will answer and say to them, 'Truly I say to you, to the extent that you did it to one of these brothers of Mine, even the least of them, you did it to Me.' **(Matthew 25:34-40)**

> 'What shall we say then? Are we to continue in sin so that grace may increase? May it never be! How shall we who died to sin still live in it? Or do you not know that all of us who have been baptised into His death?' **(Romans 6:1-3)**

> 'Is this not the fast which I choose,
> To loosen the bonds of wickedness,
> To undo the bands of the yoke,
> And to let the oppressed go free
> And break every yoke?
> "Is it not to divide your bread with the hungry
> And bring the homeless poor into the house;
> When you see the naked, to cover him;
> And not to hide yourself from your own flesh?
> Then your light will break out like the dawn,
> And your recovery will speedily spring forth;
> And your righteousness will go before you;

*The glory of the LORD will be your rear guard.'* **(Isaiah 58:6-8)**
*'Righteousness and justice are the foundation of Your throne; Loving-kindness and truth go before You.'* **(Psalm 89:14)**

**1 Corinthians 13**

*'I hate, I reject your festivals, nor do I delight in your solemn assemblies. Even though you offer up to Me burnt offerings and your grain offerings, I will not accept them and I will not even look at the peace offerings of your fatlings. Take away from Me the noise of your songs, I will not even listen to the sound of your harps. But let justice roll down like waters And righteousness like an ever-flowing stream.'* **(Amos 5:21-24)**

*'So, as those who have been chosen of God, holy and beloved, put on a heart of compassion, kindness, humility, gentleness and patience; bearing with one another, and forgiving each other, whoever has a complaint against anyone; just as the Lord forgave you, so also should you. Beyond all these things put on love, which is the perfect bond of unity.'* **(Colossians 3:12-14)**

# Chapter 9

## Pastoring people
## and taking personal responsibility

In churches we take pastoring the people seriously and with passion. We have systems and strategies planned to care for the people who make the church their home and family. It is an area in church life that for some people can save their lives and for others can cause some confusing expectations. Hopefully this chapter will bring some clarity!

In Ezekiel 34 we read God's view about the leaders who He had put into place to care for the chosen people of Israel. It's a strong and terrifying chapter that describes pastors who care for themselves and neglect their people. God was not happy. The pastors here were not good at serving their people and caring selflessly for them. In chapter 3 of this book is an overview of the centrality of servanthood as a characteristic for everyone following Jesus. Leaders and pastors are expected to model this same attitude with no exception. Jesus says about being a leader or a pastor, *'... the one who is the greatest among you must become like the youngest, and the leader like the servant...I am among you as one who serves'* (Luke 22:26-27).

Pastoring people is serving people to point them to Jesus and help them find freedom and holiness.

The mandate of the church is to serve lost people so that they may have a revelation of Jesus, experience His love, power and mercy and become free from their baggage and pain. As followers of Jesus we are also on the journey of actively *'working out our salvation with fear and trembling'* (Philippians 2:12) and therefore allowing God into more areas of our heart to continually set us free. When we pastor people we facilitate them to come on the journey of seeking to become more like Jesus and pressing into all that we are created to be.

Isaiah 61 gives us the mandate with clarity:

*'The Spirit of the Lord God is upon me because he has anointed me to preach good news to the afflicted, He has sent me to bind up the broken-hearted, to proclaim liberty to the captives...'* **(Isaiah 61:1)**

**Dependence on God**

In churches we need to be careful to avoid building a culture of dependence on people rather than God. It is the primary job of a pastor to point people to Jesus and facilitate them to find their help, wisdom, guidance and healing from Him. In an environment of fast food and quick-fix solutions it's easy to look to people to fix life's problems rather than wait on God for His answers. It can be a natural tendency to talk to the seen rather than the unseen when life is tough, yet the answers reside in God Himself. People can misunderstand the role of pastors and hope that they will give answers quickly, fix problems and take pain away. However, this is confusing the role of parent to a small baby with that of parenting young adults. With parenting young adults and pastoring, it's essential to encourage them to recognise the power of choice, consequences and personal responsibility.

In the story of the prodigal son (Luke 15) we hear of the son who takes his inheritance early and leaves home to party whilst snubbing his family background. He ends up with no money, no friends, no future and eating the food that he is feeding to the pigs. It's in this place that he has a revelation that it would be better to go home to his father's house to be a servant than remain in this place. If a well meaning pastor had visited him in the pig sty and prayed for him to know comfort and maybe offered him money, a bed and a future, he may never have been reconciled with his father. It was essential for him to endure the consequences of his bad decisions for his growth and maturity.

There are times where it is appropriate to allow people to face the reality of their bad decisions and live through some of the consequences in order to help them in the long term. We mustn't always try and fix the problems that people may face. We find this with our children as they learn about the world that they live in. We tell them that the fire is hot but when we gently lead them close enough to the fire to feel the heat, they learn faster. When they accidentally touch the outside of a mug or oven door, they learn about heat in a very tangible way. As parents we would rather that they heeded the verbal warning, but sometimes it's an essential part of their learning to have a tiny taste of the problem to help them be warned of the dangers.

It would be easier to live in a culture of blame where we avoid personal responsibility. Just like Adam and Eve it is natural for us to blame the people around us for our problems and trials. However, we need to face up to the fact that we are often living with the consequences of our own decisions. The problems that we face can also be because of other people's bad behaviour and poor choices, but in these circumstances we have to make a decision to take responsibility for our own personal consequences.

**Worshipping only God and trusting Him first**
When we look to others to answer our problems we end up looking to people instead of God. We are also reminded that we must not put leaders on a pedestal because they will surely fall off, for only Jesus should be worshipped. It's simple and can be sometimes be more natural to look to people as our main role models rather than Jesus, but this generally leads to disappointment and confusion. We can honour, respect and even admire our friends and leaders but at the same time we need to always remember that Jesus is our only ultimate hero.

Our trust should be placed firmly in Jesus because when we trust in people above Him things can go very wrong. It's a natural weakness in all of us to trust in people above God because they can sometimes feel more responsive, accessible and comforting. It's also easy to deceive ourselves that we trust in Jesus more than we really do because the people around us can become our support without us realising it. Whilst it is important to trust people and be a community of interdependent people who enjoy helping each other, it's vital that we trust firstly in Jesus. The Bible makes this abundantly clear in Jeremiah:

> 'Cursed is the man who trusts in mankind and makes flesh his strength, and whose heart turns away from the lord, for he will be like a bush in the desert and will not see prosperity when it comes, but will live in stony wastes in the wilderness, a land of salt without inhabitants. Blessed is the man who trusts in the Lord and whose trust is in the Lord. For he will be like a tree planted by the water, that

*extends its roots by a stream and will not fear when heat comes; but its leaves will be green, and it will not be anxious in a year of drought nor cease to yield fruit.'* **(Jeremiah 17: 5-8)**

These verses create a vivid image of the blessings of trusting Jesus more than other humans. It's important as leaders that we consistently encourage any people who follow us to look firstly to Jesus as their confidence, security and anchor.

**Proactive pastoring**
There is also a time when we, as a community of believers are meant to be proactive and support each other in a time of crisis as the arms and feet of Jesus. We are meant to be people who love to go the extra mile to bless and help others. We remember the story of the man who was let down through the roof for Jesus to heal. (Luke 5:17-26) I am amazed at the audacity of these friends. They must have been so full of determination and desperation to ruin a roof, lug a man up to the top and then lower him down! I often wonder if my concern over the roof and the money lost on repairs would have hindered my desire to bring a friend before Jesus. We need to be proactive and led by the Spirit to go the extra mile to see the power of God touch our friends and loved ones. We also need to know when it's best to leave them to leave it to God to reveal His power, love and mercy.

So let's be people who remember to grasp the difference between pastoring and parenting, and instead choose to take personal responsibility for our lives and help the people around us look to Jesus and trust Him and His care first.

**Questions and some Bible verses for you to study:**
When do we know when it's right to try and fix a bad situation or help another person who is struggling and how do we know when they need to take responsibility themselves?

*The story of the prodigal son.* **(Luke 15: 11-32)**

*The story of the man being let down through the roof for Jesus to heal.*
**(Luke 5: 17-39)**

*The story of the rich young ruler.* **(Luke 18:18-34)**
*'Cursed is the man who trusts in mankind and makes flesh his
strength, and whose heart turns away from the lord, for he will be
like a bush in the desert and will not see prosperity when it comes,
but will live in stony wastes in the wilderness, a land of salt without
inhabitants. Blessed is the man who trusts in the Lord and whose
trust is in the Lord. For he will be like a tree planted by the water, that
extends its roots by a stream and will not fear when heat comes; but
its leaves will be green, and it will not be anxious in a year of drought
nor cease to yield fruit.'* **(Jeremiah 17: 5-8)**

*'Each of you must take responsibility for doing the creative best you
can with your own life. Be very sure now, you who have been trained
to a self-sufficient maturity, that you enter into a generous common
life with those who have trained you, sharing all the good things that
you have and experience.'* **(Galatians 6:5-6 The Message)**

balance

# Chapter 10

## Church: being older, younger, individual and together

God is passionate about His church. In the Bible the church is referred to as His bride, (Revelation 21) with Him as the bridegroom. I don't know anyone who goes to a wedding reception and comments that the bride is OK but a little odd and ugly.

The church is designed to be an amazing multi-generational community, which in this modern day of growing reliance on internet relationships, and yet rising isolation and loneliness, is extraordinary. One of the things that makes church such a unique and beautiful organism is the way that the different generations come together in person to focus on a shared belief and love for God. It's beautiful and amazing. A group of people, who might never meet or share anything in common, meet together and love, care and support each other. The church is a community of believers who together commit to do life with Jesus in the centre.

In the midst of this God-centred community, the enemy wants to divide and confuse people, in order to minimize the impact and influence of this extraordinary expression of togetherness. We have to be on our guard to defend the vision of the church and work hard to avoid confusion around the issues that can arise. There sometimes seem to be problems in the midst of this unique multi generational community because some aspects are emphasised at different times and lack of balance seems to be communicated inadvertently. Let's look at some of these.

### The young, the old and the in-between

As a Church we are purpose driven and focused on our future, and therefore we celebrate when the seats are full of young vibrant people who are committed to building His house in the coming years. It is a beautiful thing to watch young people worship God with passion and to know that they are defending His name amongst their peers who often only use the name of Jesus as a curse. We respect, admire and love the energy and zeal of these members of our church community.

They are not just passionate, but are also able to have deep and radical revelations of God that can be extraordinary because they seek Him first. God loves to use the young. They often have less baggage and are prepared to be totally committed, radical and hungry for God and His ways. They often have more time to study the Bible and discuss the implications for their own lives. They can be fighters, overcomers and radical disciples.

> 'Let no one look down on your youthfulness, but rather in speech, conduct, love, faith and purity show yourself an example of those who believe.' **(1 Timothy 4:12)**

We are encouraged to be like the young in many ways. We are told to pursue renewal in our thoughts and our attitudes as we put on the mind of Christ. In Ephesians 4:23 it says 'Be renewed in the spirit of your mind.' The word renewed in this verse is the Greek word; 'Ananeoo' which means 'young thinking'. Everyone who follows Jesus, no matter what age, needs to be thinking in the way that the young naturally do: with enthusiasm and passion.

### The not so young
The church is also the place where people can know passion and purpose all the days of their lives. In Psalm 92:13-15 we read the consequences of committing to a church community for the long term:

> 'Planted in the house of the Lord, they will flourish in the courts of our God. They will still yield fruit in old age; they shall be full of sap and very green, to declare that the Lord is upright; He is my rock, and there is no unrighteousness in Him.'

The older members of our churches are designed to be extremely fruitful in influence and wisdom. They can speak of God's goodness through decades of trials and difficulties, successes and blessings. These stories and testimonies are to be enjoyed and honoured as we learn from them. There is no cut-off date or shelf-life destiny for people of any age.

*Do not sharply rebuke an older man, but rather appeal to him as a father, to the younger men as brothers, the older women as mothers and the younger women as sisters, in all purity.'* (**1 Timothy 5:1-2**)

So as the older members of the church reach out to father and mother the younger ones, they in turn respect and honour them. This creates a beautiful flow of relationship, which is the perfect place to raise children. Unity pleases God and when we work together to support and care for each other I believe God smiles.

As we do life together, we go on a journey of getting to know each other. We are all so unique and wonderfully made and we all have a deep desire to belong and connect to people. This need to belong is found deep inside us and is manifested by the social activities that we immerse ourselves in and the associated behaviour, clothing and language, which often inadvertently result. We celebrate being similar to others and feeling 'normal' and yet also desire to ensure that we celebrate our uniqueness and individuality. Churches should represent the diversity of God's creation, in terms of age, race, colour, style and dress sense!

### The responsibility to know our gifts and personality traits

As we journey through life, interacting with many different people, we realise that we learn, think, react and behave both similarly and differently to each other.

We know that God has plans for each person and we have a responsibility to search out all that God has planned for us to be and do. In this journey of finding our place in life, in our future plans, in the church and in the world there are some practical tools available to help us. We can find personality tests and gift inventories that may help. We have each been given spiritual gifts, personality gifts and other gifts that we hold as a unique combination. It is essential for us to find out what gifts we have been given so that we will be responsible in the way that we use them. We see in the parable of the talents that we have been given these gifts to use for others and we will be accountable to God for our effective use of them. (Matthew 25:14-30) There are also other verses that remind us of this personal responsibility.

*'Make a careful exploration of who you are and the work that you have been given and then sink yourself into that.'*
**(Galatians 6:4 The Message)**

It can be fascinating looking at the studies, which categorize our differences. To facilitate excellent teamwork, marriages and other partnerships these personality tests and categories can be helpful in clarifying subtle yet clear differences. They can be revolutionary in helping people feel more 'normal' and full of purpose and clarity. Our learning and personality differences, which had once divided us, can now be understood better and worked around to bring greater freedom in relationships and increased grace and sensitivity in teamwork and marriage.

*'Now you are Christ's body, and individually members of it. And God has appointed in the church, first apostles, second prophets, third teachers, then miracles, then gifts of healings, helps, administrations, various kinds of tongues. All are not apostles, are they? All are not prophets are they? All are not teachers are they?'*
**(1 Corinthians 12:27)**

*'As each one has received a special gift, employ it in serving one another as good stewards of the manifold grace of God.'* **(1 Peter 4:10)**

**You were born an original- don't die a copy**
We can also be relieved that we are all created as original masterpieces, which are not meant to fit any boxes exactly. Each of us carry a unique combination of gifts, skills, personality traits and learned behaviour. We all have a specific call and plan which God has destined for us before we were formed in the womb. God created us to be unique and individual and He is the creator God who delights in diversity. As we look at nature we can see God's humour and enjoyment of diversity! Why slugs and snails? Surely one slimy creature was enough? It has been said that we are all born as an original so we mustn't die as a copy.

In Ephesians 2:10 we are told of the unique plans that God has made for us:

*'For we are His workmanship, created in Christ Jesus for good works, which God prepared beforehand so that we would walk in them.'*

*'Since this is the life that we have chosen, the life of the Spirit, let us make sure that we do not just hold it as an idea in our heads or sentiment in our hearts, but work out its implications in every detail of our lives. That means that we will not compare ourselves with each other as if one were better and another worse. We have far more interesting things to do with our lives. Each one of us is an original.'* **(Galatians 5:25-26 The Message)**

### Living with purpose
When we actively seek to pursue our gifts and skills it leads us to further understand our specific purpose on Earth. We know that we are primarily called to know Him and walk with Him. We are also given the great commission from Jesus in Matthew 28:19-20:

*'Go therefore and make disciples of all the nations, baptising them in the name of the Father and the Son and the Holy Spirit, teaching them to observe all that I commanded you.'*

Jesus continually communicates His many purposes on earth and we should be able to voice ours too. Here are some of them:

*'For this reason I have been born and for this I have come into the world, to testify to the truth. Everyone who is of the truth hears my voice.'* **(John 18:37)**

*'...I came that they may have life and have it abundantly.'* **(John 10:10)**

When we live life certain of our purpose and mission, content in our uniqueness and identity, it is an adventure of being loved and loving others where we can see the kingdom of God extended, and the dominion of darkness lose its grip on people in our sphere of influence. A life with Jesus in the centre is a life of abundance, adventure, purpose and fulfilment.

**Some questions and some Bible verses to study:**
In your life right now how do you relate to those who are older than you
and how are you discipling those who are younger? Do you feel confident
of the unique role and gifts that God has given you?

'Now you are Christ's body, and individually members of it. And God
has appointed in the church, first apostles, second prophets, third
teachers, then miracles, then gifts of healing, helps, administrations,
various kinds of tongues. All are not apostles, are they? All are not
prophets are they? All are not teachers are they?'
**(1 Corinthians 12:27)**

'As each one has received a special gift, employ it in serving one another
as good stewards of the manifold grace of God.' **(1 Peter 4:10)**

'For this reason I have been born and for this I have come into the
world, to testify to the truth. Everyone who is of the truth hears my
voice.' **(John 18:37)**

'...I came that they may have life and have it abundantly.'
**(John 10:10)**

**The Parable of the Talents (Matthew 25:14-30; Luke 19:12-28)**

'This is My commandment, that you love one another, just as I have
loved you.' **(John 15:12)**

'Make a careful exploration of who you are and the work that you
have been given and then sink yourself into that. Don't compare
yourself with others. Each of you must take responsibility for doing
the creative best you can with your own life.' **(Galatians 6:4-5 The
Message)**

'Out of respect for Christ, be courteously reverent to one another.'
**(Ephesians 5:21 The Message)**

*'For we are His workmanship, created in Christ Jesus for good works, which God prepared beforehand so that we would walk in them.'* **(Ephesians 2:10)**

*'Since this is the life that we have chosen, the life of the Spirit, let us make sure that we do not just hold it as an idea in our heads or sentiment in our hearts, but work out its implications in every detail of our lives. That means that we will not compare ourselves with each other as if one were better and another worse. We have far more interesting things to do with our lives. Each one of us is an original.'* **(Galatians 5:25-26 The Message)**

Lightning Source UK Ltd.
Milton Keynes UK
UKOW05f1612230813

215871UK00001B/17/P